# Trauma-informed Care in Intellectual Disability

A self-study guide for health and social care support staff

Frankish
TRAINING

Pavilion

by Dr Pat Frankish

# Trauma-informed Care in Intellectual Disability
## A self-study guide for health and social care support staff

**Published by:**
Pavilion Publishing and Media Ltd
Blue Sky Offices
Cecil Pashley Way
Shoreham by Sea
West Sussex
BN43 5FF
Tel: 01273 434 943
Fax: 01273 227 308
Email: info@pavpub.com

Published 2019

A catalogue record for this book is available from the British Library.

ISBN: 978-1-912755-79-0

Pavilion Publishing and Media is a leading publisher of books, training materials and digital content in mental health, social care and allied fields. Pavilion and its imprints offer must-have knowledge and innovative learning solutions underpinned by sound research and professional values.

**Author:** Dr Pat Frankish
**Production editor:** Mike Benge, Pavilion Publishing & Media Ltd
**Cover design:** Emma Dawe, Pavilion Publishing & Media Ltd
**Page layout and typesetting:** Emma Dawe, Pavilion Publishing & Media Ltd
**Cover illustration:** Jo Hathaway
**Printing:** Severn Print

# Contents

# About the author

Pat Frankish is a clinical psychologist with many years of experience in the field of disability and psychotherapy. Her early life was spent living in the grounds of a long-stay hospital where her parents worked. Even as a child she knew that things could be better for the people she knew. After later working in the hospital and meeting a clinical psychologist, she secured a university place and then went on to train as a clinical psychologist. During her training she also followed a course of study in psychodynamic psychotherapy. Her career has followed a path of bringing these two areas together; her book *Disability Psychotherapy: An innovative approach to trauma-informed care* was published in 2015.

Pat continues to develop and provide services and training for staff who support people with complex needs, the group who have trauma in their background and arrested or delayed emotional development as a response.

## About this publication

The publication you are reading is one of a series of titles created by Dr Pat Frankish for those supporting children and adults who have experienced trauma, particularly those with intellectual disabilities (learning disabilities).

Currently, the series includes:

*Trauma-informed Care in Intellectual Disability: A self-study guide for health and social care support staff*

*Frankish Assessment of the Impact of Trauma in Intellectual Disability (FAIT)*

*Nought to Three – Becoming Me: A guide for parents (and those who support them)*

For full information go to www.pavpub.com/learning-disability/trauma-informed-care-in-intellectual-disability-a-self-study-guide-for-health-and-social-care-support-staff

For Pat Frankish Training go to www.frankishtraining.co.uk

# Introduction

This guide to trauma-informed care has been written for those supporting people with intellectual disabilities (ID) in any setting. Recent studies have identified that there is a high incidence and prevalence of trauma in the ID population. Some of this relates to experiences of being restrained and separated from people they know. Some of it stems from early traumatic events, and these will be the basis of much that is written here. For many years, psychotherapy has been denied to people with intellectual disabilities who have experienced trauma, on the grounds that they could not benefit from it. We know that to be untrue now, and attempts are made to redress the balance. However, individual psychotherapy will always be in short supply, so finding ways for support staff to work therapeutically has become the focus of this guide.

The content of the guide is designed for self-study by individuals and teams. It is equivalent to NVQ Level 2 learning and is based on a training course that can be accessed from Frankish Training (www.frankishtraining.co.uk). The guide covers the main topics of trauma-informed care via the theoretical positions of key researchers who have worked in either the field of psychotherapy, or disability, or both. It brings together these bodies of knowledge so that support staff can plan interventions for the benefit of the person with intellectual disabilities.

 **STOP AND THINK** There are numerous 'Stop and think' opportunities throughout the guide to help the staff member or team apply the content to their experiences. Chapter 10 considers when and how to make appropriate interventions in order to address an individual's emotional distress.

This guide can be effectively used in conjunction with the *Frankish Assessment of the Impact of Trauma in Intellectual Disability (FAIT)* assessment tool (2019) – see www.pavpub.com/health-and-social-care/health-learning-disability/frankish-assessment-of-the-impact-of-trauma-in-intellectual-disability-fait. The FAIT assesses the level of emotional development of the distressed individual, thereby allowing for an intervention to be provided at the right level. Once the stage of emotional development at which the person has become stuck has been identified, it becomes possible to work out at what age the person was traumatised. This then enables some exploration of the traumatising events and it becomes possible to consider which therapeutic theory is most useful for the individual. For example, trauma identified for a child around the age of two is often linked to the arrival of a sibling. The trauma can then be compounded by the younger sibling overtaking them developmentally. They may present to services after attacks on the younger sibling and the mother.

It is then possible to work out that the distressed child needs the level of nurture of a much younger child in order to function; providing this nurturing properly enables development and the realisation of potential. Failure to provide it takes the young person on a trajectory towards more violence, loss of freedom and more trauma. In this type of case the work of Bowlby (1998) is helpful, as is that of Winnicott (1964).

Another example would be a young woman referred for excessive self-harm and massive mood swings that appear to have no trigger. Assessment of emotional developmental stage will almost certainly arrive at less than two years old. The work of Klein on the *Depressive Position* (1998) helps us with this, both to understand and to direct the intervention appropriately.

Anyone assessed as pre-individuation on the FAIT Tool will need the security of a significant other available at all times. The additional therapeutic work is then informed by the additional theories.

Frankish, P. (2021). *Trauma-informed Care in Intellectual Disability.* © Pavilion Publishing and Media Ltd.

# Chapter 1: Infant Development and Emotional Health – The Work of Donald Winnicott

Donald Winnicott lived from 1896 to 1971 and was an extremely influential child psychoanalyst. He and other psychoanalysts working during this time were responsible for the understanding we now have that the first few years of life are vital in laying the foundations for future psychological and emotional health.

Winnicott did much of his work during World War Two, when thousands of children were separated from their parents for long periods after being evacuated from the cities for their own safety. Winnicott studied the effects of this separation on the children and was able to show how important continuity in both the physical and personal environment is for a child to grow optimally, and have the best chance of healthy development. His ideas and work are laid out in the many books and papers he wrote, some of which are listed as recommended reading at the end of this chapter, and in the final References section (see page 80).

## The model of synchrony

The theme running throughout Winnicott's books is the idea that, in order for a child to have the best possible chance of healthy and optimal development, emotional, physical and intellectual development must occur together, in 'synchrony'. This should occur in a safe and secure 'facilitating environment' – one that helps a child to reach their full potential in all three areas of development.

Winnicott's studies of evacuated children (1964) gave support to this theory, as he showed that some of those children who had delayed emotional development, due to being separated from their parents, also had difficulties with intellectual development.

From Winnicott's work, I have developed a model that looks at how the synchrony between emotional, physical and intellectual development may be affected in a child that has a disability; I also explain that these areas may develop at a different rate to each other, which is called 'dyssynchrony'.

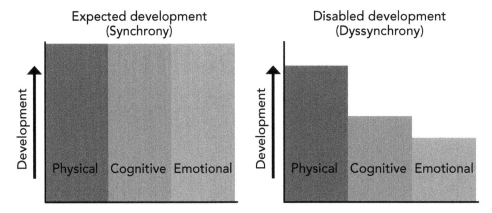

**Figure 1.1:** The developmental tasks when they are in 'synchrony', and in impaired development when they are in 'dyssynchrony'

Winnicott's work showed the importance of a child's earliest 'primary relationship', and how this can affect their development and have a lifelong impact on functioning. I have adapted these ideas to people with intellectual disabilities.

This chapter will examine the 'good enough' normal development, the consequences of difficulties in this process, and then consider how a person with disabilities may be affected.

# Normal or optimal development

Winnicott said that the most important contribution the parents, or primary carer, make in their child's development is to provide complete devotion in the first three to four years of life. The baby is born with the ability to grow and develop, but the carer is responsible for providing a suitable physical and emotional environment in which this can take place. This is called the 'facilitating environment'.

## 'Good enough mothering'

At the time Winnicott was working, the mother was usually a child's main carer and the person that they formed their earliest primary relationship with. From this fact he coined the term 'good enough mothering' to describe the conditions needed for optimum emotional development in the child. He talked about how 'good enough mothering' allows the child to feel loved and safe and secure enough to be able to develop and become an independent person.

Today, as society has changed, sometimes other people are the baby's primary carer and we now talk about the child receiving 'good enough care'. However, to keep things clear, in this chapter we will refer to 'good enough mothering' as Winnicott talked about it, but do acknowledge that it may be the father or another person with whom the baby forms the primary relationship.

## Care of a new born baby

Winnicott described that, with a newborn baby, the mother experiences something called 'maternal pre-occupation', where she is completely pre-occupied with meeting the needs of her baby. This is something that happens naturally and intuitively. The pair become completely enmeshed, to the extent that, as Winnicott stated (1964):

*'There's no such thing as a baby – but a nursing pair.'*

By this he meant that the baby and the mother are an interdependent unit because the baby cannot survive without the protection, love, security and food that the mother offers.

The baby is not a passive recipient in this process. It is the baby's energy that causes the mother to respond to its needs. The mother and baby visually interact with each other and will gaze into each other's eyes. The baby will also make 'spontaneous gestures' meaning that it does something that the mother responds to, the baby then responds back and the mother responds and so on. This is the baby's first experience of interaction with another human being. In an ideal situation, this stage of 'maternal pre-occupation' will be supported by the partner or family so the mother can focus solely on the baby's needs.

During this early stage the baby only really experiences the world as consisting of itself and the primary carer, and is unable to distinguish that they are separate beings. As the mother is so preoccupied with meeting the baby's needs the baby feels it is 'omnipotent'. This means that the baby feels it is at the very centre of existence, and believes that it is in charge. For example, when the baby feels hungry and wants to be fed, it cries and the bottle or breast appears. The baby then thinks that it's hunger and desire to be fed has made this happen. Winnicott called this the 'illusion of omnipotence' because it is, of course, an illusion.

During this early period the primary carer processes the baby's extreme, intense emotional states. If the baby is feeling upset, tired, hungry or scared it may become extremely distressed. The carer then tries to find the source of the distress and to offer comfort. In this way the parent processes the baby's difficult emotions which stops it from being overwhelmed by them, as at this stage the baby does not have the ability to deal with the emotions itself. The parent learns to 'tune in' to the baby's needs and emotional states and can begin to identify the meaning of different cries. The parent's ability to tolerate these extreme emotions without feeling rejected by the child is important, so that they can continue to be able to process the emotions for the baby.

It is through this primary relationship and receiving 'good enough care', that the baby's 'ego' or sense of self begins to develop. The Ego is a term introduced by Freud (1927) that will be covered in a later chapter, but it basically means the personality or 'person we are'. In a newborn child, the Ego is unintegrated and the baby experiences a mass of sensations from the world around it. At this stage the baby does not have a strong enough Ego to enter into relationships with other people. It only has the primary relationship with the mother or primary carer.

Winnicott described how 'the baby sees itself reflected in its mother's eyes', because in an ideal situation the baby will see love and joy reflected there. It is this warm, loving and positive feedback that allows the baby's Ego to integrate and a strong and positive sense of its self being 'good enough' to develop.

If the primary carer is able to:

■ respond to the baby's needs

■ tolerate its 'omnipotence' or need to be the centre of existence

■ process the child's extreme emotions

■ stop the child from being overwhelmed

■ give positive feedback

it will all help the child to feel safe and secure and allows its sense of self, or Ego, to begin to develop.

## Moving on from 'maternal preoccupation'

As the baby gets a little older the mother begins to move out of the 'maternal pre-occupation' stage and starts to return to being a person in her own right, and is not so enmeshed with her child. She may not be quite as 'tuned in' to the baby's needs and may not meet them as immediately as was done previously. Through

Frankish, P. (2021). *Trauma-informed Care in Intellectual Disability.* © Pavilion Publishing and Media Ltd.

this, the baby learns to tolerate difficult feelings such as frustration and anger at sometimes having to wait for its needs to be met.

Through this process the baby begins to realise that the mother or carer is a separate being from itself, and from this begins to develop the sense that there is a world outside of the enmeshed mother and baby unit. The baby begins to develop a sense of 'what's me and what's not me' – i.e. the difference between itself and the world outside.

Once there is a sense of a world outside itself, together with its needs not always being met immediately, the baby's sense of omnipotence begins to lessen as it feels that it is no longer at the centre of the universe. The mother helps the baby deal with the difficult emotions of frustration, anger and fear that it can't control the world and that everything it desires doesn't always happen. All this helps to strengthen the baby's Ego, develop its sense of self and becomes the foundation for developing independence.

Through this 'good enough' primary relationship, and getting feedback that it is 'a good enough child', the baby is able to establish a strong enough Ego and sense of self to be able to relate to others. The child then begins to enter into interactions with other people, such as the other parent, grandparents or siblings. From this the baby then progresses to being able to explore the wider world.

It is through this process of gradual separation from being enmeshed that the good enough mother or carer helps the baby to learn to tolerate the separation, as well as the frustration of not having its needs met immediately, in small digestible steps, so that it is not overwhelmed. In this way the good enough mother gradually builds up the baby's ability to tolerate difficult feelings, again strengthening the Ego and sense of itself that it is 'good enough' and therefore gradually helping independence.

This process lays down the building blocks and foundations for happy and healthy mental health later in life. Winnicott used the term 'good enough mother' as a contrast with the 'perfect mother' who would try to meet all of the baby's needs immediately, but in doing so would stop or delay the baby developing a sense of self as a separate being and also stop the baby from being able to tolerate frustrations.

## Transitional object

As the mother begins and continues this process of separating herself from the enmeshed relationship with the baby, the baby may take a 'transitional object', known to parents the world over as a 'security blanket' – which may or may not be a blanket. To the baby, this dearly held object, which may be an old piece of cloth or teddy bear, represents the safety and security of the mother or carer. Having the transitional object while away from the carer allows the child to bear the anxiety of being separated.

 **STOP AND THINK** about your own transitional object – try and remember what it was and if you remember how you felt if you ever lost it. Or think about how a child you know and what its transitional object is – how has that child reacted to losing it?

Have you worked with any adults with disabilities that may have been very attached to a particular object? How have they reacted if this has been taken away?

This may have been a transitional object that was deemed as not age appropriate.

# Intellectual development

As the child begins this gradual separation from the primary carer and is able to enter into other relationships and explore the world, it begins to be able to think about itself and the world. The child becomes aware of the 'what's me and what's not me?' boundary; or the difference between itself and the rest of the world.

Through the process of visual interaction, the baby monitors the primary carer's reactions to get a sense of whether it is safe to explore in different situations. It is only able to do this through the absolute trust it has in the carer to keep it safe. Through its explorations, the baby begins to deal with or rationalise the information coming into its brain through its senses.

Through this process the child gradually learns to be able to think, and then this progresses to being able to 'think about' things. The baby begins to be able to 'cathect', or hold in its own head, a reality of its world on a day-to-day basis. When it comes across something new, the child relates the new information to what it is already holding in its head. It has reached the stage of 'rationalisation', where it can think about itself and its environment.

It is the trust, interaction, safety and security of the primary relationship that allows the child to first develop this ability to think, and then the ability to 'think about the world' through its exploring and having relationships with other people.

Frankish, P. (2021). *Trauma-informed Care in Intellectual Disability*. © Pavilion Publishing and Media Ltd.

The child needs to have these experiences to be able to think, and then 'think about' the world and reach the point of rationalisation.

# Development of the 'true self'

Winnicott (1964) said that when a child receives 'good enough care' the sense of self it develops is its 'true self'. That is, if the baby has had its needs met and has received love and a sense that it is 'good enough' from its carers, its personality can grow and develop just as it is, so the child can show its 'true self' to the world.

Children that don't receive this can develop a 'false self', discussed in greater detail later. This can occur when a child develops in response to what the primary carer and, later, other people, want, and therefore the 'sense of self' it develops is not the baby's true sense of self, but rather what other people want it to be – a 'false self'.

Winnicott described how people who are able to develop and present to the world a 'true self' feel energised, creative, glad to be alive and have a sense of 'wholeness' or 'completeness'.

# When things go wrong – when care is not 'good enough'

So far we have covered the ideal caring situation that helps a child to have the best chance of developing to its full potential. Sometimes, however, a child does not receive this ideal 'good enough parenting' for whole host of reasons.

 **STOP AND THINK** about and list the reasons why a parent may not be able to provide 'good enough' care.

Some of the reasons why a parent may be unable to provide good enough care include:

- The mother and the baby are separated.
- The mother may not be able to give the maternal nurturing the baby needs due to her own difficulties, such as mental health problems.
- The parents may feel completely overwhelmed in their new roles as parents, or may not have enough support to help them.
- The mother may suffer from post-natal depression, a very severe condition that needs effective treatment and can affect the mother's ability to relate to her child.

# What happens to a baby that does not receive 'good enough' care

In a situation in which a baby does not receive 'good enough care', the primary carer may not be able to read the baby's needs and/or emotions. They may not be able to tolerate the demands of the baby, or cope with its omnipotence and its need to be the centre of everything. The mother may be unable to respond to the baby's spontaneous gestures or enter into a state of being joyful with it. The carer may be unable to process the baby's emotions, leaving the child completely overwhelmed by them.

If the mother is unable to respond to the baby naturally, the child may then be unable to respond to her. As this pattern becomes entrenched, the baby may become fractious and irritable, which can disappear but re-appear later, in a more serious form of behaviour. In severe cases, when care is 'not good enough' there can be rejection of the baby or even child abuse.

 **STOP AND THINK** about what a baby in this situation may see reflected in its mother's eyes and give details of how this will affect its sense of self.

In a situation where the baby does not receive good enough care, the child will not receive the feedback it needs that it is itself 'good enough'. The basic building blocks of personality have been interfered with and this can have a massive impact on the child, leading to personality or Ego disturbance.

In reality, most people fall between receiving the perfect, optimal mothering experience and the not-good-enough mothering experience.

## Consequences of not receiving good enough care

### True self/false self

If the baby's spontaneous gestures are not responded to or its needs are not met, the baby will begin to comply with what the mother wants, who will then respond more positively to the baby when it does what she wants, rather than what it wants. This may make it easier for the carer to manage the baby. However, for the baby, compliance to what the carer wants means suppressing its own needs. As this continues over time the baby suppresses its 'true self' and begins building up a 'false self'. This 'false self' is based on the baby complying with what the carer wants, rather than what the baby needs.

Frankish, P. (2021). *Trauma-informed Care in Intellectual Disability.* © Pavilion Publishing and Media Ltd.

This 'false self' can then go on to become the 'self' or personality that is presented to the world. The person themselves may not even realise this is their 'false self' as it has become so ingrained over the years. The 'false self' becomes so entrenched because it is a way of defending or protecting the 'true self' that wasn't nurtured or responded to.

Someone who is presenting a 'false self' to the world can often have a sense of not really being alive, feelings of unreality and the feeling that happiness doesn't really exist. These people may be vulnerable to breakdown if the appropriate environmental trigger occurs. The person may have the whole of their personality development affected or they may 'fixate' or 'stay' emotionally at the stage where they were failed in their mothering.

## Delays in intellectual development

As the process of being safe and secure enough to explore the world and other relationships does not start, or does not get completed, the child may suffer in their intellectual development. The child may not develop an interest in the outside world. They may not receive enough stimulation, which will have a dramatic effect on intellectual development.

## Compulsive self-reliance

Another consequence of being 'let down' in the nurturing experience and not receiving 'good enough care' is that the child may start to feel that they can't trust the primary carer and may instead start to rely on themselves and their own judgement at too early an age. It is appropriate for a child of five or six to begin to trust their own judgement, but at the age of 18 months or two years it is very problematic and leads to lifelong consequences of the person being 'compulsively self-reliant' and too dependent on themselves.

This can affect their future life and relationships, as the child doesn't learn how to seek help from others in an appropriate way. In later life the person may not be able to ask for help when they need it as they can't bear to be dependent on anyone else. These people do get through life, but often need to use all their emotional energy to keep themselves independent and self-reliant.

## Other consequences

Other consequences of the failure of 'good enough parenting' are the child or adult showing a lack of self-confidence, being anxious or fearful that they won't be listened to, and feeling that their needs don't count. This is unsurprising if their needs were consistently not met as a baby and young child. This failure in the primary relationship can leave people feeling fearful of everything in life as the child has not had the opportunity to develop a strong sense of self and self-confidence.

Another consequence may be behaviour problems as the child behaves in a way to demand the attention that it craves but isn't receiving. For the child, even if they receive an angry response to their behaviour, this feels better for them than being ignored because at least their existence is being acknowledged.

Sometimes the primary carer may have been over-protective. They may have continued to meet the child's every need and not have been able to give the child what was needed to increase their sense of self, independence and confidence in the outside world. This may result in a person who is over dependent on others and has never really achieved a sense of being independent and confident in the world.

If the child has had poor levels of attention and contact they may end up with poor communication skills, as they have not had the necessary opportunities to learn them. This can then go on to affect intellectual development. They may also have difficulties relating to others and have relationship problems. The person may end up using their behaviour as the main way of communicating their needs.

## Extreme consequences

In terms of more extreme consequences of failed parenting, Winnicott (1990) writes about the link between delinquent or criminal behaviours and early deprivation in the primary relationship, and talks about the type of crime or delinquent behaviour a person shows being linked to the type of deprivation that they experienced as a child.

Another very serious consequence can be a fear of women, especially if the mother was very hostile towards the child. This can lead to 'misogyny' or hatred of women. In extreme cases it has been found that many rapists and murderers of women have had failed relationships with their mother and were sometimes later abused by a woman.

In very extreme cases a person may develop a psychopathic personality. If a baby has been grossly neglected or left on its own for long periods of time and rarely had its needs met, it may not develop the ability to relate to other people. In its most severe form, this could eventually lead them becoming psychopathic or antisocial and amoral, not caring about other people or their needs or emotions.

To sum up: if parenting fails and the child does not receive 'good enough care' then the basic building blocks and foundations for a robust sense of self and good future mental health are not laid down, through no fault of the child. The child may be left to struggle through life the best it can with the basic personality or Ego having been distorted in some way. This can lead them to struggle with challenges in life and leave them vulnerable to later stress and mental health difficulties.

Frankish, P. (2021). *Trauma-informed Care in Intellectual Disability.* © Pavilion Publishing and Media Ltd.

# Children with disabilities

So far we have discussed what needs to happen for optimal development and robust mental health and functioning as an adult. We have looked at why this sometimes fails and what the consequences may be. In a child with learning disabilities the situation can become even more complicated. Often, the child, because of the disability, is less able to receive 'good enough parenting', even if it is available.

 **STOP AND THINK** about why a child with disabilities may have difficulties receiving 'good enough parenting'. Make a list of some of these difficulties.

Children with disabilities, through the best of intentions, may have frequent separations from care givers. They may need hospitalisation, or may attend a Child Development Centre or nursery at a younger age than their peers, with the aim of helping their cognitive development. They may have respite care with the intention of helping the parents to deal with the additional stresses of having a child with disabilities.

This separation will affect the child's sense of security and their ability to attach to care givers and engage in that so-important loving, one-to-one relationship. Also, if there are lots of separations the child will have a loss of the 'facilitating environment' it needs as it moves from place to place. This will affect the feeling of security and safety the child needs for their development.

Having a child with disability can sometimes be a devastating experience for parents, which can impact on their own emotional functioning. The care of a disabled child can be more stressful than caring for a non-disabled child. There are usually many more issues to deal with and also possibly lots of professionals involved. This can make it more difficult for the child to receive the optimal caring it needs.

Because of the disability it is often difficult for a parent to 'tune into' a disabled child. The child may be floppy, may cry a lot or may be difficult to feed. This will affect the parent's ability to recognise, understand and meet the child's needs. The parents may not be able to recognise or respond to the child's 'spontaneous gestures' and engage in the 'reverie' that helps the child's development of sense of self. It can, sadly, sometimes be hard for a parent to love a disabled child and give the care needed.

If the parent is not able to meet the child's needs, then the child may later use behaviours to get their needs met, leading to entrenched challenging behaviours later in life, or the child may give up trying to communicate its needs, becoming passive and retreating into its own world.

A child with disabilities may not be able to engage in the physical movement needed in bonding such as running after the parent when they leave the room. This may lead to the child being left alone more often because the parent is not so worried about the child moving off and hurting itself. A child with disabilities may also not have the physical resources available to hold onto a transitional object. They may not be able to kick up a fuss and scream and shout if the object is removed or they lose it. The child then doesn't have the experience of the manageable or 'bit by bit' separation from the carer. This can cause the child to be overwhelmed by anxiety and can lead to them growing up feeling unable to trust others.

Sometimes the parents of a disabled child may become very overprotective and may not be able to move on from the 'maternal preoccupation stage', and consequently the child doesn't have the opportunity to grow more independent.

In his book *Playing and Reality* (1971), Winnicott talked about play being an important part of development and not just something to fill in the time. It is the way that children learn to have control over the world and is important for all areas of development. Games that the child plays with care givers help with bonding. If the child is physically disabled they may not be able to take part in playing in a way that helps them to develop.

 **STOP AND THINK** and give details about how someone you know or work with, with disabilities, may have been affected by their disability in terms of being able to access 'good enough parenting' and whether any of their experiences/factors that you know of may have affected this.

## How this affects synchrony in developmental tasks

Returning to Winnicott's Model of Synchrony between the developmental tasks, we have seen how difficulties in a child's primary relationship will affect its ability to receive 'good enough' care. In a child with disabilities, the disability may impact on their ability to receive the good enough care, even if it is available and the parents are trying their very best.

This is likely to lead to 'dyssynchrony' in the developmental tasks, which is where emotional development is not able to happen or is arrested. This can then have a knock-on effect on the child's intellectual development, and in extreme cases even their physical development. This all causes the child's development to be compromised, leading to further difficulties in later life.

# How therapy can help

Therapy can help an adult by reproducing the 'good enough' primary relationship that they missed out on as a child. This doesn't mean holding or hugging the person, but by being consistent and reliable and being able to tolerate the client's difficult emotions of pain, anger and distress, the therapist can give the client some of the experiences that they didn't get in the primary relationship, but which are needed for emotional development. The therapist is able to respond to a person's emotional needs while being completely unconditional and being able to 'hold' the person's distress or behaviour.

Over time, the person begins to trust the therapist, begins to value their opinion, and at this stage they can begin to explore relevant issues. A therapist may need to see someone for several months to establish this 'good enough' therapeutic relationship before beginning the actual therapeutic work. This is often called the 'pre-therapy relationship'.

If a person has become 'stuck' or 'arrested' in their emotional development, the therapist can establish exactly the stage at which this happened. The therapist can then help the person to grow emotionally by enabling them to have access to the support that they didn't get in the primary relationship, but which is needed at that stage of their development.

Therapists working with people with learning disabilities often have the experience of seeing a person develop during therapy not only emotionally but also intellectually. This often happens because, if a person is being able to develop emotionally, it may help their intellectual development as well. In this way the person is then moving forwards in their developmental tasks, even if this is much later in life.

# Chapter 2: Attachment and a Secure Base – The Work of John Bowlby

John Bowlby worked in the 1960s and 70s and was a colleague of Winnicott. He is famous for his work on attachment and wrote a number of books on the topic that have now been printed together in a book called *A Secure Base* (1988). His ideas have influenced present day ideas about child care and children going into hospital.

## Affectional bonds and attachment

Bowlby wrote that human beings have a natural tendency, or 'drive', to make 'affectional bonds' with other people, meaning close and intimate connections with others. Having a bond leads to attachment between two people. Making affectional bonds is the basic foundation of human social and emotional life.

 **STOP AND THINK** about how bonds and attachments are the basis of emotional and social human experience.

List the types of relationships where bonds are needed.

Until relatively late in the 20th Century, it was a common belief that babies do not begin to form attachments until they are about one year old. Bowlby disagreed with this, and described how a newborn baby will begin to make 'proximal bonds' i.e. bonds to those nearest to it, which is usually the parents, right at the beginning of life. Once such a bond has been made it will stay solid and strong and last for a lifetime. The first bonds that a child makes are called the 'primary attachments'. These attachments are vital for the survival of the baby, who needs the parent to nurture and care for it.

If a child makes good, strong primary attachments, they will then be able to make attachments and bonds with other people throughout life. Therefore, the process of attachment is another vital building block for robust mental health and emotional well-being in life. Disturbances in this attachment process can lead to difficulties relating to others and forming relationships, which can lead to emotional and psychological problems.

For a good, strong, positive primary attachment to be made, the primary carer needs to be available and present enough for the child to make the attachment. They need to be consistent, reliable, positive and encouraging in their relationship with the child. This enables the child to feel safe and secure in its attachment to the primary care giver. It is the quality of the emotional relationship that is important, not what the child is given in terms of the material trappings of family life such as food and toys.

This secure attachment is the optimal or most beneficial form of attachment style, and it helps the child to develop a robust sense of self and of being 'good enough', enabling the child to relate to other people and form healthy relationships later in life.

# A secure base

Once the primary attachment has been made and the child feels safe and secure in this relationship, they have what Bowlby called 'a secure base', sometimes known as the 'safe base'. This is not a place, but is the actual relationship in which the child feels safe and secure. Location is not as important as two people being together and feeling enough regard and affection for each other to form an attachment.

From this 'secure base' the child feels safe enough to explore the world, knowing that it has the secure base relationship to return to. This idea is very similar to what Winnicott said about the 'good enough mother' helping the child to feel secure enough to explore the world.

 **STOP AND THINK** about how a young child, when starting to become independent, will move away from the parent to explore but keep looking back at the parent to check they are there, and then sometimes run back. This is an example of a child returning to its 'safe base'.

# Growing independence

Bowlby said that 'the aim of attachment was to detach' (1988). What he meant by this was that if the child has made a strong affectional bond with its primary care giver, it will eventually go through the process, when growing up, of separating and becoming independent from the primary care giver, and will then be able to attach to other people in adult life such as friends, partners and children.

It is not possible for the child to be independent and separate in a healthy way as an adult if they have not first been attached and then detached from their primary care giver. The building blocks of a healthy sense of self in relation to another person, i.e. the primary relationship, have to be in place and strong enough before the child can go on to make other healthy relationships.

## Benefits of secure primary attachment

A good, strong and secure attachment will enable the child to make good, strong attachments throughout the rest of their lives and will help them to make healthy relationships later in life. They will be self-reliant and have the self-confidence to think, 'I'm alright, I'm an OK person and I'm able to live an OK life'. This sense of being comfortable with oneself comes from having a strong enough attachment, with positive feedback as a young child.

It is important to distinguish this self-reliance from the 'compulsive self-reliance' that Winnicott talked about, discussed earlier, in which the person is only able to rely on themselves and not on others, to the extent this then becomes problematic for them.

People who have had good primary attachments are able to work and collaborate with others. They are self-confident and self-reliant enough not to be threatened in group situations and therefore make good 'team players'; they are able to 'give and take'. They have a personality that is 'interdependent', meaning that they are neither overdependent on others, nor too independent. As a result, they can work in an interdependent, collaborative way with others.

## Attachment maps

In adult life we continue to need good attachments with people for whom we feel mutual affection and respect, and with whom we feel able to be ourselves and be accepted as ourselves. For most people, the optimum number of people needed to have this kind of attachment with is between six and ten people. If these attachments are drawn out this is called an 'attachment map'.

**STOP AND THINK** about your own attachment map. Draw a large circle and put your name in the middle. Now draw in the circle people that you feel you are attached to. Put the names of those you feel closest to nearest to your name.

Now repeat this exercise for someone you know with learning disabilities.

You will probably find they have many less people in their attachment map, or that the people in their maps or near the centre are paid to be in their lives.

Think about how a person with learning disabilities may feel about the carers who are paid to be in their lives.

# Separation

Bowlby noticed that if a child's primary attachment figure is missing, the child will go through a number of distinct stages. Initially, they will 'protest' very loudly, demanding to know where the person is. The child then moves into the next stage of 'despair', becoming very distressed, and will scream and cry. They will not be comforted by others. After some time however, if the attachment figure has not returned, the child will then move into a state where they appear not to notice the person is missing or that it doesn't matter.

In the past this was often interpreted by people as the child being at ease with the separation. However, Bowlby found that the child was actually moving into a stage of 'mourning' or depression at the loss of the attachment figure. At this stage, in the child's mind, they have 'given up' and have accepted the fact that they've been abandoned.

Often when the attachment figure returns, the child initially feels insecure about their return and is unsure whether or not they will be abandoned again. However, if the child is securely attached, this will usually soon pass and the child will be relatively easy to comfort and will show joy at the person returning. It is important that the child is helped to process their feelings about this separation and is reassured, or there is a danger that the child may be left with anxiety problems.

 **STOP AND THINK** about how, before Bowlby's work, when a child went to hospital it was procedure for the parents to be encouraged to leave them, not stay with them or visit them too often. Sometimes the child may have been in hospital for long periods.

How do you think this may have affected those children?

Due to Bowlby's work, parents are now encouraged to stay with children or at least visit as much as possible, with many wards providing sleeping facilities for parents or having open visiting hours.

# Insecure attachment

Attachment is a crucial building block in psychological development, and the consequences of these attachments not being secure or of affectional bonds being broken are huge.

For the child to make an attachment bond to a parent, the parent needs to be reliable, consistent and physically around enough for the bond to occur. If the child does not receive this, their attachment will be insecure or not formed at all. If a child does not have a secure attachment, then they do not have a safe base from which to explore and enter into the wider world.

A child that is insecurely attached will often react differently to separation in that they will go to anyone who is available. Because they are not secure in their attachment, they don't recognise that it is only some people who provide the safe base and security and that other people don't. Consequently, they will often go to anybody, which can make them very vulnerable.

Often insecurely attached children are also very 'clingy', as if they are trying to 'hang on' to the person they are with. They may also find going to nursery or school difficult because they do not have the certainty in their mind that the parent or the secure base (i.e. mum being at home) will still be there at the end of the day.

A child who has an insecure attachment style will not have as much self-confidence as a child who has been securely attached. They may not have a robust sense of being 'OK' or 'good enough'. They often find it hard to 'give and take' in relationships. In adulthood, these people may find it difficult to attach to other people. They may be superficial in their relationships or be very possessive due to not being able to give and take.

Sometimes people may become very 'martyr' like, always trying to be there for and help other people before themselves. The drive for this is that by being acknowledged or thanked for their help, they are being 'seen' or 'noticed', an experience that they probably didn't get enough of as a child. This type of person is often seen in the caring services as they are driven by a pathological need to care for other people.

## Permanent separation

Bowlby identified that the period from 15 to 30 months is the most crucial period for maintaining the consistent presence of the attachment figure to allow strong, secure attachments to build. Now able to walk, this is the stage in which the child is beginning to explore the world. But in these explorations they need the secure base to go back to. If the safe base or attachment figure is not there, they will stop exploring the world, become depressed and won't engage with other people.

We have already looked at the stages a child goes through when they are separated from their primary attachment figure. However, if at this crucial age the separation lasts longer than six months or happens repeatedly, or if the separation is permanent due to a tragedy, then the child enters a stage of 'pathological mourning'. They won't be able to attach to other people and will become very separate and independent of other people, or detached from them. Being at this point is often called being 'permanently detached'. It is unlikely that without help they will ever recover from this enough to be able to make further attachments in later life.

This state of 'permanent detachment' or 'pathological mourning' can often be seen in adults if they have had serious separations in childhood or have been taken into care and had to leave their primary attachment figures. In this state of pathological mourning people just accept loss, without the mixed emotions that usually accompany a loss. Often there is a 'flatness' about them as they repress the anger, despair and sadness that would normally be seen in dealing with a loss.

In adulthood these people will find it very difficult to engage in relationships and there is often an absence of love and friendship in their relationships. They may be given a diagnosis of 'depression' or 'borderline personality disorder', but what is actually happening is a permanent state of mourning for the 'lost self', or the person they would have been if the affectional bond had not been broken too soon.

# Pathological parenting

Some people, even though primary care givers have been available to them as a child, suffer psychological difficulties and distress because of the way the parents have been with them as a child. Bowlby called this 'pathological parenting', because it is the way the child has been parented that has led to them experiencing psychological distress in life.

## Unresponsive, negative parents

It is not enough for the parent to just be there, they also need to be responsive and positive towards the child. If parents are consistently unresponsive to the child or rejecting or negative, a child can be left thinking there is something wrong with them. Small children, especially, are not able to rationalise what is happening or to understand its parents' behaviours and will just take on board how the parent behaves towards them, which will have an impact on the child's ability to grow up and see itself as a 'good enough person'.

## Inconsistent parenting

If a parent or primary attachment figure 'comes and goes', either through illness or for other reasons, the child is left in a state of not knowing whether the parent

Frankish, P. (2021). *Trauma-informed Care in Intellectual Disability.* © Pavilion Publishing and Media Ltd.

is going to be reliable or not. They will wonder if the parent is going to be there in the morning, or the next week. This will have a huge impact on their ability to be secure in their attachments and therefore their ability to grow and develop.

## Making threats

Sometimes when disciplining a misbehaving child a parent might make threats such as 'I won't love you anymore if you carry on behaving like this'. Of course, the parent does not actually mean what they say, however if these threats are made often enough the child can begin to take them seriously. This may leave the child with a sense that they are 'not lovable', and this sense can be taken into adulthood and affect their future well-being.

Continual threats that are conditional, for example 'I'll only love you if you're good' or 'I'll only love you if you're clean', can lead to the child and later the adult, desperately trying to be 'good enough' to be loved. This can sometimes lead to distorted or obsessive behaviours such as excessive cleaning.

## Threats to abandon

Again, it is common to hear a parent saying to a small child, 'If you don't behave, I will leave you here' or, 'If you don't come now, I'm going without you', in an attempt to try and get a child to comply. Most parents don't mean it, however some do and will actually leave the child.

This threat of being abandoned, if it occurs regularly, or is carried out, is more than a child can take psychologically and as a consequence they may become very clingy or run around after people. In later life they may be very dependent on others or be very fearful of being abandoned and left alone. Sometimes as adults, people stay in unhealthy or damaging relationships because they cannot bear to be alone.

## Threats to kill, harm or commit suicide

'You'll be the death of me', 'Looking after you is killing me', 'If you do that again, I'll kill you', are things that, again, a child might hear but is unable to rationalise. The child is unable to think about what is going on for the parent to make them say such things. This leaves the child with hearing comments that have a detrimental effect on their sense of self and their development.

## Blaming

Similarly, statements that blame the child and make them feel guilty, such as 'you've driven me to this' or 'you've made me ill', put enormous pressure on a young child and will have an impact on their psychological and emotional development and their mental health.

Pathological parenting can have a major effect on a child. It can affect their sense of self and the person they become later in life. It can affect their future relationships – both friendships and intimate relationships – and can also have an impact on their relationships with their own children. Children may be left going through life carrying a feeling that they are not good enough, not loveable, or with immense guilt. The tragedy of this is that they were good enough and lovable to start with, but it is the parenting they have received that has left them with these difficulties.

# Attachment and people with disabilities

A disabled child's ability to attach to a primary care giver may be affected in many ways. Firstly, the child may have frequent separations from the primary care giver due to respite care or stays in hospital. They may not get enough consistent time with the parent to be able to make an attachment. The very disability itself, especially if it is physical, may affect the child's ability to stay in close proximity and chase after the parent or follow them if they leave the room. From the parent's point of view this may be a relief as they do not have to be so vigilant of the child's whereabouts, but it can have a lasting impact on the child's ability to attach to the primary carer. In addition to this, a physical disability that affects mobility may affect the child's ability to explore the world from the safe base.

## Parenting a child with disabilities

Becoming a parent is a massive change in any person's life. It can at times feel extremely stressful and overwhelming. Having a child with disabilities can increase this stress and worry. Additionally, the parents may be grieving for the 'perfect child' they thought they would have and can struggle to come to terms with the disability. In these circumstances it can be hard for parents just to keep going. Under this stress parents may end up resorting to saying things that they don't mean, the types of things that Bowlby described as 'pathological parenting'.

If the child has learning disabilities, they will have even less understanding of why the parent is saying these things or be less likely to be able to rationalise the situation. This will lead to them being in an even more insecure position with potential interference in the development of the sense of self.

# Parents with learning disabilities

Society often thinks that adults with learning disabilities do not have the skills and abilities needed to be parents. This can result in their children being taken into care, which can be devastating for the parents. It can also obviously be massively damaging for the child. Due to the awareness of the importance of affectional bonds, and the consequences for the child of being taken into care, services now work much harder at supporting parents with learning disabilities to care for their children, so the child can remain with them and doesn't have to have a broken affectional bond.

# Bowlby therapy

A person may come to therapy because they are in some kind of distress. This sometimes can be due to failed parenting, even if this has not been deliberate. Most parents do the best they can at the time but unfortunately people get ill, divorces happen or they have other life pressures to deal with. Therapy is not about blaming the parents. It is about looking at what happened to the person and how they have been affected by their experience, especially their ability to form relationships and relate to people.

Therapy helps the person process their experience in the family and what they did to survive or cope. Often, people take with them into adulthood ways of coping that helped them survive as a child but which are no longer working for them or are causing additional problems. If a person can gain insight into this, they can then begin to make some changes in their life and relationships.

By being reliable, consistent, positive and unconditional, the therapist will enable the therapeutic relationship to become a 'safe secure base' for the person, an experience they may not have had before. Within this therapeutic relationship, the person can then begin to explore what's happening in their lives now and where this has come from. If the person has insight and understanding of why they keep getting into unhealthy or damaging relationships or harmful patterns of behaviour they can then begin to choose different ways of being that stop them from repeating the pattern.

Bowlby gave hope that it is possible to repair some of the damage caused by attachment difficulties, as long as the personality has not been completely destroyed. If the person is able to form some sort of attachment in therapy they may gain great benefits from this. However, for some people, their attachment has been so pathological that they are simply left without the capacity to make strong affectional bonds and attachments. This is a very sad situation and one that cannot be changed. However, therapy can offer these people the opportunity to understand this and why it has happened. Once they have this understanding they may be able to 'learn to live' with this reality and accommodate it into their way of life.

## People with disabilities in therapy

People with disabilities commonly don't have many people in their lives to whom they are securely attached. We have discussed previously that most people need between six and ten people with whom they can attach and be known and accepted for themselves. For many people with learning disabilities this number is often much less. A person's closest relationships may be with those staff who are paid to care for them, who unfortunately may leave for other jobs.

For the client, during the time of therapy, the therapist may become the most important person in their lives. The therapist may be the main person in their lives giving them positive feedback and enabling them to develop a sense of self as a 'good enough' person.

The work of Bowlby and Winnicott gives us a model of how a supportive emotional environment and therapy may repair some of the psychological and emotional damage caused by poor early experiences. By enabling the person to experience at least some of the things they missed in early life, they can be helped in their emotional development and we now know that this can also help with intellectual development.

# The work of Winnicott and Bowlby – some final thoughts

Bowlby and Winnicott have both had a huge impact on our present day understanding of how vitally important the early years of life are in setting us up for good lifelong psychological health.

Recent research has highlighted this further. In 1989, in Romania, many orphanages were discovered where children had been abandoned because their parents could not afford to care for them. These orphanages were woefully understaffed and often the children received very little or no attention and spent their days alone in their cots. It was found that the children had massive emotional, physical and cognitive problems as they grew up. They were unable to form attachments and relationships or relate to other people. Recently, many of these children have been followed up and been found to have taken these difficulties into adulthood (psychologyhub.co.uk). Interestingly, the children who shared a cot with another child have fared better – probably because they were at least able to have some contact with another human being.

In 2004, Sue Gerhardt wrote a book called *Why Love Matters*, which discusses recent research undertaken by scientists looking at the effects of attachment and early relationships on the brain, using brain imaging technology. It has been shown that love and touch actually stimulate the brain to grow and the connections in the brain to develop.

It has been shown that the brains of children who did not receive good enough parenting or had poor attachments develop differently. The connections between the brain cells are affected, as is the part of the brain that controls stress and mood. This can lead to developmental difficulties for the child and also leave them more vulnerable to stress and mental health problems in later life. This can leave the child going into adulthood with brains that are more prone to depression and other mental health problems.

The work of Winnicott and Bowlby has also affected government policy in allowing mothers a year of maternity leave and encouraging paternity leave, so the baby can form those close and hugely important primary relationships with its parents.

# Chapter 3: Biological Birth to Psychological Birth – the Work of Margaret Mahler

Margaret Mahler worked as a psychoanalyst in the United States in the 1970s. She set up a laboratory to observe children from birth to five years old with their primary carers. Through these observations Mahler was able to understand the stages of emotional development that a child goes through. She was also able to describe the behaviours seen at each stage.

Mahler wrote up this work in a book called *The Psychological Birth of the Human Infant*, published in 1975. This book describes the stages from biological birth or when the baby is born, through to the child's 'psychological birth'. This is the point the child has an individual identity of its own, which usually happens around three and a half years old. Mahler called this 'psychological birth' the point of *individuation*. This is very similar to what Winnicott described as 'rationalisation'. This is when the child has gone through the emotional developmental stages and can think clearly about itself within its environment.

I have adapted Mahler's work to thinking about people with a learning disability. I describe how people can become 'stuck' at certain stages of emotional development. This chapter will firstly look at Mahler's stages in neurotypical development. Then we will look at how this applies to people with a learning disability and how to assess someone's emotional development stage. We will then look at how to put interventions into place so that a person's emotional development can be supported and nurtured.

# Overview of Mahler's stages of development

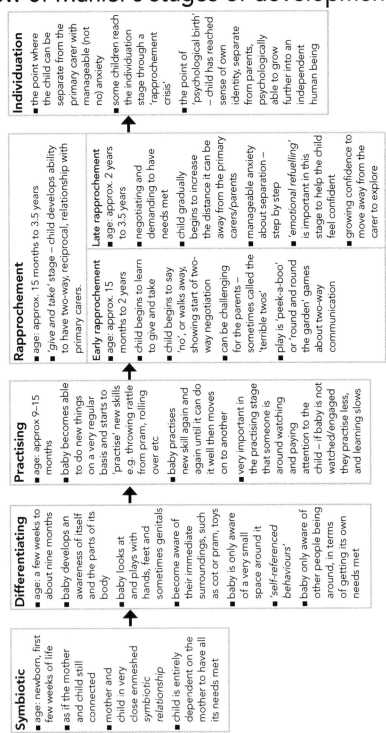

**Symbiotic**
- age: newborn, first few weeks of life
- as if the mother and child still connected
- mother and child in very close enmeshed *symbiotic relationship*
- child is entirely dependent on the mother to have all its needs met

**Differentiating**
- age: a few weeks to about nine months
- baby develops an awareness of itself and the parts of its body
- baby looks at and plays with hands, feet and sometimes genitals
- become aware of their immediate surroundings, such as cot or pram, toys
- baby is only aware of a very small space around it *'self-referenced behaviours'*
- baby only aware of other people being around, in terms of getting its own needs met

**Practising**
- age: approx 9–15 months
- baby becomes able to do new things on a very regular basis and starts to 'practise' new skills e.g. throwing rattle from pram, rolling over etc
- baby practises new skill again and again until it can do it well then moves on to another
- very important in the practising stage that someone is around watching and paying attention to the child – if baby is not watched/engaged they practise less, and learning slows

**Rapprochement**
- age: approx. 15 months to 3.5 years
- *'give and take' stage* – child develops ability to have two-way, reciprocal, relationship with primary carers.

**Early rapprochement**
- age: approx. 15 months to 2 years
- child begins to learn to give and take
- child begins to say 'no', or walks away, showing start of two-way negotiation
- can be challenging for the parents – sometimes called the 'terrible twos'
- play is 'peek-a-boo' or 'round and round the garden' games about two-way communication

**Late rapprochement**
- age: approx. 2 years to 3.5 years
- negotiating and demanding to have needs met
- child gradually begins to increase the distance it can be away from the primary carers/parents
- manageable anxiety about separation – step by step
- *'emotional refuelling'* is important in this stage to help the child feel confident
- growing confidence to move away from the carer to explore

**Individuation**
- the point where the child can be separate from the primary carer with manageable (not no) anxiety
- some children reach the individuation stage through a 'rapprochement crisis'
- the point of 'psychological birth' – child has reached sense of own identity, separate from parents, psychologically able to grow further into an independent human being

**Figure 3.1:** The road to individuation

Frankish, P. (2021). *Trauma-informed Care in Intellectual Disability.* © Pavilion Publishing and Media Ltd.

## Symbiotic stage

The *symbiotic stage* is the newborn phase in the first few weeks of life. At this stage it is as if the mother and child were still connected. This is the stage that Mahler *et al* (1975) described, when the mother and child are in the very close enmeshed relationship. It is called the *symbiotic relationship*. In the symbiotic stage the child is entirely dependent on the mother to have all its needs met.

## Differentiation stage

The *differentiation stage* is when the baby develops an awareness of itself and the parts of its body. This stage starts at a few weeks old and goes to about nine months. At this stage babies will look at and play with their hands, feet and sometimes their genitals. They also become aware of their immediate surroundings, such as the cot or pram that they are in, and the toys that are around them. At this stage the baby is only aware of a very small space around it and is beginning to notice that it exists within this small space.

The behaviours seen in the differentiation stage are called *'self-referenced behaviours'*. This means that everything the baby does is about, or in reference to, itself. It doesn't do anything to influence anybody else. Although if the baby screams or cries this will influence others – the reason the baby does it is because it wants something for itself i.e. is hungry or cold. The baby is therefore only aware of other people being around in terms of getting its own needs met.

## Practising stage

Brain development in babies happens very quickly. As a result, the baby becomes able to do new things on a very regular basis. Mahler found that the baby will start to 'practise' a new skill as it becomes available. The baby will practise the new skill again and again until it can do it well. Examples of this would be the baby throwing a rattle out of the pram and doing so again and again. Other behaviours would be learning to roll over, crawling and standing up.

This stage begins at around nine months and continues to around 15 months. The baby may practise behaviours at other times but this is the main *practising stage*. When the child can do a particular behaviour well, another becomes available due to the brain's rapid development. The child then begins practising this new behaviour.

It is very important in the practising stage that someone is around watching and paying attention to the child. Mahler found that if the child knew it was being watched, then the practising behaviour continued. If the child thought that nobody was paying attention they practised much less. This would make learning a new behaviour much slower.

## Rapprochement stage

The word rapprochement means *'give and take'*. Give and take is one of the most important skills needed in relationships. In this stage the child is beginning to have a two-way, or reciprocal, relationship with its primary carers. This stage is divided into two sub-stages – early rapprochement, and late rapprochement. It goes from about 15 months to about three and a half years.

## Early rapprochement

The early rapprochement stage is the start of the child beginning to learn to give and take. This begins around 15 months and goes on until about two years. The first sign that a child has moved into the early rapprochement stage is when the child begins to say 'no', or walks away. This shows the start of two-way negotiation. The child moving into this stage can be challenging for the parents and is sometimes called the 'terrible twos'.

In this stage the child will become interested in 'peek-a-boo' or 'round and round the garden' games. These games are about two-way communication and give and take between two people.

## Late rapprochement

The *late rapprochement stage* is the beginning of the child moving towards independence. This stage can be more challenging as the child is negotiating and can be demanding in getting its needs met. This happens from two to three years.

In this stage the child also gradually begins to increase the distance it can be away from the primary carers or parents. It can do this with its levels of anxiety being manageable. This is similar to the ideas of Winnicott and Bowlby, who talked about the child gradually having the confidence to move away from the mother or 'safe base' and explore the world.

It is really important that the child's anxiety is manageable so they are not overwhelmed. Independence grows in small steps that the child can cope with. For example at play group the child may start off being sat by its mother's feet. When it is a few months older the child will move away to play with the other children in the middle of the floor. It can do this by being able to keep an eye on mum and where she is. As the child moves into late rapprochement it will be able to go a bit further away from mum. It can do this without being anxious about where she is.

'*Emotional refuelling*' is important in this stage to help the child feel confident. This is where the child will look round for the parent and make eye contact. This eye contact will 'emotionally refuel' the child and help them feel confident. They can then happily carry on playing at a distance from the carer.

By having the confidence to move away from the carer the child can begin to explore and through this the child is learning about the world around it. The child is also beginning to understand its own place in the world.

## Individuation stage

Once the child has moved fairly smoothly through the stages above it reaches the *individuation stage*. This is the point where the child can be separate from the primary carer with manageable anxiety. Note: this is not a state of having no anxiety – it is normal and indeed sometimes helpful to have some manageable anxiety. It is instead a state of not being overwhelmed by anxiety when separated from the parent or primary carer.

Some children reach the individuation stage through a 'rapprochement crisis'. This is when they realise the primary carer is not there, they become anxious, distressed and may have a tantrum. They then realise that they can cope with the situation. Individuation is the point at which they child knows that they are separate from the carer but that they can manage the anxiety of this.

Reaching the individuation stage is the 'psychological birth' of the child. It is the point at which they have reached their own identity, as being separate from their parents. At this point the child is psychologically able to grow further into an independent human being, who can stand on their own two feet.

Margaret Mahler helps us to understand the stages that a child goes through to reach individuation. She helps us to know what behaviours can be seen at each stage. It is therefore possible, by observing the behaviour of a child, to work out what stage of emotional development they are at.

 **STOP AND THINK** about a child you know and relate the information you have just read to them. Think about how their behaviours changed as they went through these stages.

# The role of the primary carers in this process

The primary carer or parent is crucial in helping the child move through the stages of emotional development. They are the person that keeps re-appearing and meets the child's needs in the differentiation stage. In the practising stage, the carer is the person who encourages the practising behaviours by taking notice of what is happening. In the rapprochement stage the carer is the person with whom the child develops its interaction and negotiation skills. It is also in this stage that the carer is reliably there for 'emotional refuelling' so the child can begin to explore the world and become increasingly independent.

# When things go wrong

Unfortunately, a lot of people don't go through all of these stages and may become 'stuck' at a stage of emotional development. This can happen due to some difficulty in their primary relationship and not receiving 'good enough care'. It may also happen due to a traumatic separation from the primary carer. Sometimes a child may be placed into the care system and have multiple carers. The child doesn't have the constancy of the primary carer that they need to develop through the stages.

It is extremely rare for someone to get stuck at the symbiotic stage, although it is possible. If someone gets stuck at the differentiation stage, they do not develop the ability to relate to other people in a meaningful two-way interaction. They would have been able to do this if they had developed to the rapprochement stage. Their potential for becoming happy, healthy, useful adults is very limited. These people will be vulnerable to severe personality disorders or psychotic illnesses in later life.

People stuck at the practising stage may end up with conditions where they engage in repetitive behaviours. These are sometimes called *'safety behaviours'*, as they serve to keep the world around the person just the same. These safety behaviours help the person to feel safe. A person stuck in the practising stage may be more vulnerable to conditions such as obsessive compulsive disorder, autism, borderline personality disorder or bipolar affective disorder.

A person stuck at the early rapprochement stage will be less ill than someone stuck at an earlier stage. They may be able to carry on a 'normal life'. However, they are often anxious, worried people, dependent on those around them to keep them feeling safe in the world.

Those people who become stuck in the late rapprochement stage can be very demanding. They expect other people to meet their needs all the time. They can be quite dominant, as they want everything around them to be just so.

 Frankish, P. (2021). *Trauma-informed Care in Intellectual Disability.* © Pavilion Publishing and Media Ltd.

The ideal and most healthy position for people to reach is the individuation stage. People who have reached this stage can engage in healthy, meaningful two-way interactions with other people that are balanced. This links to Winnicott's idea about people who have a 'good enough' sense of self and are able to be 'interdependent'. This means that they are neither too independent nor dependent. They are able to engage in healthy, 'give and take' relationships and can fully function in the world.

# How this relates to people with learning disabilities

I have developed a way of using Mahler's theories to understand people with learning disabilities. In the 1980s I worked in a long stay learning disability hospital. I noticed that many of the behaviours of the adults there were similar to the stages of emotional development that Mahler had described. For example, I noted that some people were totally self-absorbed. They might be sitting in a chair sucking their fingers and playing with their clothing. They were absorbed with their own body and their own chair. They were often not aware of other people or staff around. I noticed that these behaviours were very similar to the *self-referenced behaviours* that Mahler had described in the *differentiation stage*.

I also noticed that many people showed behaviours such as pacing and rocking. Some people showed more severe behaviours such as skin picking or head banging. These behaviours are often called *stereotypical behaviours*. They were very common when people lived in the old large institutions. These behaviours were often thought to be ways the person could stimulate themselves. I, however, thought that these behaviours could be seen as *practising behaviours*, as would be seen in the *practising stage*.

I also saw some people showing behaviours described as 'attention seeking'. They might be screaming out for staff or following staff around or throwing things so that staff had to come to them. These were behaviours that would keep other people involved with them. This *'attention-seeking behaviour'* was seen by staff as being a negative thing and a nuisance. I thought that these behaviours were similar to those you might see in the *early rapprochement stage*. I thought that the people doing these behaviours were aware that other people around could meet their needs. They were therefore doing these behaviours to try and get their needs met.

I noted that people who seemed to be in the *late rapprochement stage* were often the ones considered to be 'a real nuisance'. This was because they knew that their needs could be met and they were determined to get them met. These people would be the ones who were trying to get staff members to engage with them all the time.

**It is perhaps significant that I noted that there did not appear to be anyone in the long stay hospitals who had reached the *individuation stage*.**

At this time, in the 1980s, it was thought that any difficult behaviours a person showed were part of the person's disability or condition. However, we have already seen during these chapters how children with disabilities may not to be able to make use of, or receive the 'good enough' parenting and secure attachments needed for emotional development. It makes sense that a failure in this would lead to the person becoming 'stuck' in their emotional development.

I set out to understand whether these behaviours were in fact due to a person being 'stuck' at a stage of emotional development and being unable to develop further. I did this by firstly observing people's behaviour to find the stage of emotional development they were at. I then put in place an intervention which gave the person what they needed at their particular stage of emotional development. I then observed to see if this intervention had helped the person to move onto further stages of emotional development.

We will now examine the observation method that I developed and then look at individual therapeutic interventions and staff interventions.

# How to establish a person's emotional stage

I have devised an observation method which shows a person's emotional developmental stage. It is more complex than just watching someone. It can be done in 40 minutes. Later in this book there are more details about how to do this; you may also use the FAIT Tool, included in Chapter 8 of this self-study guide. In this chapter we will just outline how this observation is done.

## How to undertake an observation

In a 40-minute observation, the observer would watch the person for 20 seconds. In the next 40 seconds they would write down exactly what they had seen in those 20 seconds. It would take exactly one minute to observe and write down. The information collected is called a 'data point'. This process is repeated over 40 minutes and the observer collects information for 40 'data points'.

To learn how to do these observations properly takes practice. There may be a huge amount to observe in the 20 seconds and it can take practice to 'tune into' a person's behaviours.

The data collected is then analysed to look for the most common type of behaviour i.e. whether it is self-referenced, practising or reciprocal, 'give and take' behaviours. The most common type of behaviour would determine at what level of emotional development the person is.

It is extremely rare to find anyone at the symbiotic stage so this stage can be discounted; people at the individuation stage are likely to be doing fine and not need this type of observation, so this stage can also be discounted.

Therefore, data is analysed at the four remaining stages:

- differentiation
- practising
- early rapprochement
- late rapprochement.

The most common behaviours seen at each data point would be given a number 1–4, for the stage the behaviours represent. When these are counted up, one stage will dominate. This is the stage the person is mostly at.

You may find it helpful to read the following information in conjunction with the Observer sheet templates and examples provided in Chapter 8, pages 74 and 75.

## Apparent anomalies

Occasionally, behaviours may be seen that belong to another stage. For example, you may see a few practising behaviours when most of the ratings show the person is at the differentiation stage. This indicates that the person is beginning to move into the next stage, or can be helped to do so.

 **STOP AND THINK** about doing some informal observations. You could plan to observe either someone you support or a child you know. Try watching a person and 'tuning into' their behaviours and what they are doing. Think and detail what stage these behaviours are at, given what you have just read.

> ## Same behaviour, different meanings
>
> A crucial factor in this theory is to recognise that the same behaviour can have different meanings, depending at what emotional stage the person is at.
>
> Same behaviour, different meaning – head banging
>
> - Someone head banging who is at the differentiation stage would be doing it as a self-referenced behaviour or for self-stimulation.
> - If the person is at the practising stage, they may head bang because they can, and haven't yet developed another behaviour to replace it.
> - At the early rapprochement stage, a person is likely to be head banging because they are trying to communicate something such as 'I want someone to give me some attention'.
> - At the late rapprochement stage, the person's head banging is likely to be more controlling, meaning 'you better get here quick or I'm going to do something worse'.

Quite often, simple behavioural approaches may recommend ignoring an unwanted behaviour. This is because it is thought that paying attention to a behaviour makes it happen more. However, this means a person stuck in their development does not get the presence of the significant person that they need. This means they are not able to develop emotionally and move through the stages.

# Designing interventions

Prior to this work the emotional development of people with learning disabilities was often not thought about. Even today the focus of intervention is often to teach people new skills and appropriate behaviours. There is often no consideration of whether a person's stage of emotional development would enable them to learn these new skills.

Using Mahler's ideas, I understood that the key thing in any intervention is the need for the active presence of a significant other person. However, the type of engagement needed varies depending on which stage the person is at. They need from the significant person what they would have got from the primary carer, but didn't get, because the relationship was disrupted in some way.

## Example:

### What is required from a care giver

Someone in the differentiation stage needs someone just to be present to respond to their self-referenced behaviours and meet their needs.

At the practising stage it is the presence of someone to practise the behaviours in front of that is required.

At the rapprochement stage the important thing it is the presence of someone who the person can develop interaction skills with.

# Individual therapy

Initially, I did this intervention work through individual therapy. The therapist would provide the person with the type of engagement they needed at their emotional stage.

### Supporting John

John is a young man. I observed John and found that most of his behaviours were self-referenced, although he did have a few practising behaviours. I found that he was stuck in the differentiation stage. When I reviewed John's history, he had had some traumatic experiences when he was a young baby. He seemed to have become stuck emotionally at the stage he was at, when the trauma happened.

Therapy initially involved me just being present in the room with John. This was because what John needed at the differentiation stage was someone to be consistently present to meet his needs. Over time John began to show interest in objects in the room and began practising behaviours with them. I would show interest in this and help him to keep practising. I then helped him learn different practising behaviours. He was eventually able to move into the early rapprochement stage. At this point John was more interested in interacting with me.

John did not reach the individuation stage due to the severity of his early experiences. However, life was much easier for him in the rapprochement stage. He was now able to have two-way interactions and relate to other people.

I recognised that if it were only therapists who provided this type of intervention the number of people able to receive it would be very limited. I then developed interventions so that a nurturing emotional environment can also be provided by staff teams and families. This now means that a lot more people can benefit from appropriate emotional support and can grow and develop emotionally.

I published a paper of this work of adapting Mahler's theories to people with learning disabilities. It was published in 1989 and is listed at the end of this section. The paper described how to provide a therapeutic environment which gives the person the right emotional support for the stage they are at. By doing this it is possible to nurture and help a person's emotional development.

## Designing a staff or family intervention

We already know the importance of the presence of a primary carer in early emotional development. This is vitally important up until about three years of age or when the child reaches the individuation stage. Therefore the 24/7 presence of a primary or significant carer is the key issue in the development of any staff interventions.

In caring sectors it is not possible for a paid member of staff to be there all of the time. However, staff just being 'around' or having a team of staff working with a group of people is not enough to encourage someone's emotional development. To replicate the presence of a primary carer the person needs to know that they have a staff member who is available for them.

A way around this is to put in place a rota that has a small group of named workers for the person. Therefore, in any 24/7 period the person knows who their named worker is. They know the person who is available for them. This enables the person to establish a good attachment with all of the staff in the small group of named workers. Staff handover needs to be in the presence of the client. This allows the person to know who is going to be there for them on the next shift or in the morning.

The approach works better if the named carer can be the one that provides the food and does the caring tasks as well. This is because it replicates what happens in the primary relationship. However, if the staff member doesn't do this, the most important thing is that the person knows that their carer is there for support if they need them. It is important to stress that the staff do not have to be in immediate contact with the person all the time. What is important is the person knowing where the staff member is and, if they go away, when they are coming back.

Once this system is put in place there is often a very quick reduction in the person's anxiety. This is because they know every minute of the day that there is someone there for them. There is also usually an increase in that person's cooperation and adaptive behaviour.

### Resistance to this type of support

In learning disability services, there is often a resistance to allowing clients to become attached to staff. It is seen as a bad thing. Services worry about clients becoming too dependent on staff and how they will cope if staff leave.

In services where attaching to staff is discouraged there are still often people desperate to hang on to a particular staff member. These tend to be the people who are most afraid of being alone. This doesn't mean there's something about that particular staff member that the person is attached to. It is because they know they can hang on to that staff member and they won't be pushed away. It happens because they desperately need to have somebody. These people are the ones who are often very distressed at staff changeover times. It is not about the person being demanding or manipulative, as is often thought.

It must be remembered that this approach is based on the absolute basic need for a person to know that someone is there for them. It is about meeting this most essential need, in terms of emotional development. If staff are there for someone in a way that meets their emotional needs, the person will become more independent as they develop emotionally. Eventually they will not need the same level of support.

## When the relationship with the primary carer is established

The next stage in the intervention is to introduce some activities that are appropriate to the person's emotional development stage. If someone is at the differentiation stage then it is appropriate to try and introduce some practising behaviours to the person. This can be sensory things that they can experience and try out. This may be things like building bricks, sand or water activities or objects they can squeeze.

Once the person is engaged then it is important to encourage them to practise with something until they are competent. At this point another activity can be introduced which they will practise until they are competent at that. By doing this the person is gradually increasing their repertoire of behaviours. The aim is to move them on until they are solidly in the practising stage.

When the person is in the practising stage, activities can be introduced to move the person onto the early rapprochement stage. This may be things like 'peek a boo' games or passing a ball to each other. This is to help the person develop their skills in two-way interaction.

It is also appropriate at this early rapprochement stage to talk to the person about their environment. By doing this the carer is developing their interest in the world by describing and pointing out the colours and names of things. This will help the person to see what is going on in the world around them and develop their interest. It also helps to build the person's relationship with their primary carer. This all helps the person to become more interactive with the world around them, including other people.

In the early rapprochement stage a person's quality of life is greatly improved. They can begin to relate to other people and will be more curious about the world. Because of this, their potential for experiencing and learning about the world increases massively.

If the person is well established in early rapprochement it may be possible to help them move to late rapprochement. The work here would be to help them to communicate their needs. Through this they will then be able to get into negotiation with another person and begin to bargain. This two-way communication and give and take is what mature adult life is all about.

## When someone is inbetween stages

It may have been noticed in the observations that someone was mainly at one stage but still had some behaviours at the next stage. In this case it is extremely important to gear interventions to the earlier level. This is because trying to get the person to engage in an activity they are not ready for is punitive for the person. We are working with people who may only be 12 months old emotionally, which makes them very vulnerable. If they are nearly ready to move to the next stage and interventions are put in at the lower stage, it just means that they are ready to move on more quickly.

## How Mahler's approach would fit in a group home

A lot of challenging behaviour is often thought to be manipulative in nature or the person trying to get own way and may be ignored for this reason. However, we can now see that the behaviour is indicating that the person may be at a much earlier emotional development stage than previously considered – they may very well not have reached the stage of being able to be demanding or manipulative.
In addition to this, in a small group home that uses behavioural techniques, people would probably be on programmes that reward or reinforce appropriate behaviours but ignore inappropriate behaviours.

It must be recognised that for a person who is not yet at the individuation stage, their behaviours are occurring to get an emotional need met. If the behaviour is ignored, as would happen in the above approaches, the behaviour will just become stronger because the person won't be able to process being ignored. They will carry on doing the same behaviour over and over until there is some resolution of it.

In a home using a Mahler approach, someone showing difficult behaviours will get a lot of attention. But everyone else will be getting a lot of attention, a lot of the time because they need it. Therefore everyone's needs will be met. The kind of attention given will be different depending on the level that a person is at.

## Supporting Sabine

Sabine is sat at a table banging a plate. If Sabine is known to be at the differentiation stage, the behaviour will be recognised as being self-referencing – Sabine is doing it to get a need met, that she needs help with feeding. The significant staff would say 'I'll help you with that' and meet Sabine's needs around feeding.

If banging the plate is recognised as part of Sabine's practising behaviour, then the staff would say 'here's your knife and fork, let's see if we can do it properly' and help develop the skill.

If Sabine has been assessed as being in the early rapprochement stage, the staff would respond to the behaviour by asking 'what is it you want?'

If Sabine has been assessed as being in the late rapprochement stage, staff may say something like 'You know better than that, Sabine – go and sort it out for yourself – take the plate to the sink'.

**The response given to the behaviour will vary depending on the *meaning* of the behaviour rather than the behaviour itself.**

In a house not using this approach the plate banging may be ignored. For a person at the differentiation, practising or early rapprochement stage, being ignored will be experienced by them as if they are invisible; this will likely increase their frustration, make them feel as if they don't matter, and their behaviour will then deteriorate and escalate. Alternatively, the person may be expected to act as if they were at the individuation stage and know what to do with the plate, i.e. take it to the sink, when they may not have reached that stage yet.

So we can see how crucial it is to be able to assess correctly at what emotional stage of development a person is, and respond appropriately to it. If we get it wrong, it is felt as persecutory by the person and this may also lead to behaviour worsening.

People whose behaviours worsen and become more extreme may end up in more and more restrictive environments because of their behaviour. Very often the worst thing that could happen to them is ending up in a restricted environment, in a group setting, without enough staff to meet their needs.

By providing people with support appropriate to their emotional development level we can help the person develop and grow as an individual. Providing people with this more appropriate support would stop their behaviours worsening and hopefully lead to them needing less support in the future. Apart from the obvious personal benefits to the individual, this would also be much cheaper than care provided in a secure unit.

# Chapter 4: Discovering the Unconscious – The work of Sigmund Freud

Sigmund Freud (1856-1939) is often called the 'father of psychoanalysis'. He worked mainly with adults and was the first person to really try and understand and analyse why human beings behave the ways we do. His discoveries and ideas have completely changed the way we view ourselves and our relationships with others.

## The importance of the early years

Through his work with adults and talking to them about their lives, Freud was one of the first people to recognise the importance of the early childhood experiences. He recognised how vulnerable a young child is psychologically in the first few years of life and how experiences at this crucial time can have an impact on the rest of life.

His ideas led to Winnicott and Bowlby doing the work we have already covered about just how vitally important the early years and the primary relationship and attachments are.

## Id, Ego and Super Ego

Freud developed a model to understand the inner workings of the mind. He believed that our mental or inner world is made of up of three parts which develops during childhood:

### 1. The Id
The 'Id' drives us to seek out pleasure, desires instant gratification to selfish needs. It is the part of our makeup that drives us to do things that may not be socially acceptable.

### 2. The Ego
The Ego is the part of the mind that we think of as 'the self'. It is the part that deals with the external reality of our world. It is the competent part of ourselves – our personality and the part that relates to other people.

### 3. The Super Ego

This part is better known as our conscience. The Super Ego keeps the Id under control in order for the Ego to be able to function in the world. The Super Ego gives us our sense of right and wrong. It is the part of us that ensures we act in ways that are acceptable to society rather than fulfilling our selfish needs.

Freud gave us the basic idea that we are made up of parts that together make us whole. This text has covered how our early experiences help the 'self' or 'Ego' to form.

Freud believed the Ego is very vulnerable to being damaged by any traumas the child experiences. The aim of psychotherapy based on Freud's ideas is to strengthen the ego and make it more independent of the Super Ego. In other words, to make the mind more balanced.

 **STOP AND THINK** – Think about the Id, Ego and Super Ego in relation to your own experience. Try and think about times when the Id or Super Ego has been dominant and how this affected your behaviour.

# The unconscious

Freud was the first to identify that we are not conscious of a large part of our mental life. He realised that a huge amount happens 'below the surface' in our minds. He called this our 'unconscious', as we are not conscious or 'aware' of the mental activity that happens here.

Freud understood that the unconscious can interfere with our conscious mind and can affect the things we do and say in ways we are not aware of, because we are not consciously aware of them. One aim of psychotherapy is to make us more aware of things in the unconscious that affect how we function. By becoming aware we can then choose to behave differently.

 **STOP AND THINK** about times you may have been affected by your unconscious. Are you aware of doing or saying things that you didn't mean to but actually were truthful in the situation? These are sometimes referred to as 'Freudian slips' because they are moments in which your unconscious influences your behaviour.

# Dream

Freud discovered that our unconscious is very active in our dreams and we often dream about things that are really important to us. Very often our dreams do not

Frankish, P. (2021). *Trauma-informed Care in Intellectual Disability.* © Pavilion Publishing and Media Ltd.

appear to make sense because they have come from the unconscious part of our mind, but therapists often work with a person's dreams as a way of discovering more about what is going on in the unconscious.

# Repression

Repression is the process of pushing into the unconscious difficult experiences or feelings so we are no longer conscious or aware of them. By pushing something into the unconscious mind the person does not feel the same emotional distress. This is called a *'defence mechanism'* because it 'defends' the person or protects them from emotional pain or difficult feelings.

In childhood, repression is used as a defence mechanism to protect the child from experiencing the pain of a trauma so powerfully. What this means is that the child may be able to repress or push down the extremely painful and powerful emotions that children experience when they suffer a trauma. However, these experiences and emotions are likely to resurface at some point in later life. They often do so in a way that causes the person difficulties in functioning and may cause them distress.

One of the aims of psychotherapy may be to very carefully and gently recover repressed experiences and help the person to process them so that they no longer cause difficulties.

# Transference

Transference is the process where the client 'transfers' feelings about other people in their lives onto the therapist. Often, these are very difficult feelings that the person is not able to express because they are not consciously aware of them. They may start to relate to the therapist as if they were the person the feelings were originally about.

One of the aims of psychotherapy is for the therapist to recognise this process and to help the person become aware of and express these feelings and come to terms with what has caused them.

# Drives

Freud also identified a number of what he called *'drives'*. These can be thought of as instincts that drive us to act and behave in certain ways. The two most fundamental drives he talked about is the *'death wish'*, which is a negative drive, and a positive drive Freud called the *'love wish'*.

The death wish is an instinct to go towards the depths of depression and death. The 'love wish' is the instinct or drive to find love and happiness, be with other people and have relationships.

Freud described how in happy people these two drives are in balance. One does not outweigh the other. Often people who are very unhappy may have an imbalance in the drives. Bipolar affective disorder (or 'manic depression') can be seen as a swinging between the two drives. One of the aims of psychotherapy is to help a person find a balance between the different drives.

## Conclusion

Freud was the first person to really try and understand what makes human beings behave as they do. His ideas have inspired others to develop ways of working with distressed people that underpin disability psychotherapy work today. The discoveries that he made, only some of which we have touched upon, continue to inform the way therapists work with people when trying to help a person become less distressed.

Frankish, P. (2021). *Trauma-informed Care in Intellectual Disability.* © Pavilion Publishing and Media Ltd.

# Chapter 5: The Importance of Very Early Development – Ideas from Melanie Klein

Melanie Klein (1856 to 1939) was inspired by the ideas of Freud and did much of her work with children using toys and observing how they played with them. From her work, she concluded that emotional development begins much earlier than Freud thought, starting even before we are born. Klein believed that the baby is born with what she called a 'murderous rage', probably due to the unpleasant and traumatic experience of being born.

She believed that the baby's rage and anger becomes 'socialised' or manageable through the relationship with the parent or significant other. This is very similar to Winnicott's later ideas about the importance of the primary relationship where the carer processes and contains the child's emotions.

Klein also believed the Ego existed at birth, unlike Freud who thought it formed through childhood. Klein said that the main activity of the Ego in infancy is to defend the child against anxiety by using two unconscious processes called *introjection* and *projection*.

 **STOP AND THINK** – Give two examples of the similarity between the work of Klein and Winnicott's ideas concerning significant others and primary relationships.

## Introjection

This word means 'taking in'. Klein used it to describe how the child would 'take in' experiences they had had and these experiences would become 'internal objects' in the child's inner world. Klein said that a crucial factor in a child's development was them 'taking in' their positive experience of the mother which would then represent a 'good' and dependable internal object. This process helps to strengthen the child's Ego. Unfortunately, if the child is exposed to poor or traumatic experiences these are also taken in and become 'bad objects' in the child's inner world.

Very distressed and disturbed people may have more internal 'bad objects' than good. Part of the work of therapy is to help the person 'take in' or introject their experience of the good relationship with the therapist to help balance out the bad objects they have.

# Projection

Projection is a process that happens because the baby is emotionally unable to cope with the fact that good and bad experiences can come from the same person. In the case of the mother or primary carer, this would be being fed and feeling satisfied as the good experience or not being fed immediately and feeling hungry being the bad experience. Klein believed that the baby deals with this by 'splitting' its experience of the mother into good and bad experiences. The baby experiences the 'good mother' and 'bad mother' as if she is two different people.

The baby then copes with this by 'holding onto' and internalising the experience of the good mother and 'projecting out' or pushing out the experience of the 'bad mother'. This process of splitting experiences and taking in the good parts and pushing out the bad parts continues as the baby experiences the world.

In normal development the baby's Ego is able to get stronger as it has used this process to protect against experiencing anxiety. Eventually, the baby is able to reach the point where it is able to notice and deal with the fact that good and bad feelings can come from the same person or experience.

This process is fundamental to being able to accept the good and bad parts of ourselves and other people and see people as whole. This ability to tolerate both the good and bad of a person, or experience, is one of the basic elements needed for psychological stability and mental health.

# Projective identification

This is the process where the split off part of a person, or experience, or 'bad object', is not just projected or pushed out of the inner world but is actually put onto another person. This person is then treated as if they were the 'bad object' or bad person.

Frankish, P. (2021). *Trauma-informed Care in Intellectual Disability*. © Pavilion Publishing and Media Ltd.

This process can be very useful in therapy. An example would be if a client has been abused in the past, they will have taken in and internalised that experience of the abuser as a 'bad object'. They may then, in therapy, project this bad internal object onto the therapist and start to relate to them as if they were the abuser.

This is very useful for the therapist, especially if the person is not able to talk about their experiences. When this happens, it helps the therapist to understand the person's inner world and previous experiences, and therefore help the person.

# Klein's model of emotional development

Using the ideas above, Klein described how babies, in normal development move from what she called the *'paranoid schizoid position'* to the *'depressive position'*. Klein used the word 'position' rather than stage because these positions are not fixed. A person can move between them at any point in life when emotional difficulties occur.

## Paranoid schizoid position

This is the position where the child is unable to integrate the good and bad parts of themselves or others as described above. They deal with this by 'splitting off' and 'projecting' these bad parts onto others. However, this way of coping leads them to feel that the world is full of bad people or experiences.

If the child is not able to develop and stays in this position or, as an adult, returns to it at times of emotional distress, they often see and feel things in 'extremes', either being good or bad. They can also think that the world is full of bad things and have a strong sense of paranoia.

## Depressive position

If the child is able to receive 'good enough care' from the parents it is able to work through the paranoid schizoid position and move into the depressive position. This is when the child realises and is able to tolerate the fact that good and bad things can belong in the same person. They realise themselves that they are made of good and bad parts. Sometimes this can bring difficult feelings accepting that we have both good and bad parts. However, with 'good enough' support the child is able to tolerate this and reaches the position of 'resolution' of the depressive position. This is a more mature position and way of seeing the reality of the world.

As discussed above, we move between positions throughout life when affected by emotional issues. One of the aims of therapy with distressed people is to help them move out of the paranoid schizoid position to a resolution of the depressive position.

# How this relates to people with learning disabilities

I have developed the ideas of Klein in my work with people with disabilities, especially those who are unable to talk about their experiences. I have developed the use of projective identification as a vital tool in therapy. By the therapist really tuning into and listening to their own feelings when they are with the client, they can work out which feelings are genuinely theirs and which are actually being projected onto them by the client.

If the therapist can 'tune into' the projected feelings this gives them a really good insight into the type of experiences and relationships that the person has had in their life. This is especially useful if the client is not be able to talk about things or has repressed the experiences into the unconscious and can't remember them.

By using this tool in therapy it is possible to get a much clearer sense of someone's experiences. The therapist can then begin to work with the person very carefully to help bring these experiences into the conscious. They can then help the person to process and deal with the experiences.

This helps the person to reach a position of having a more robust sense of self. It also helps the person to be able to move to the more mature resolution of the depressive position. Furthermore, the experience of therapy will help the person to 'take in' and internalise the good experience of the therapeutic relationship.

 **STOP AND THINK** about the way in which Klein's work and that described above are helpful in your setting.

How might you be able to help a client who refuses to, or can't, speak about their experiences?

 **STOP AND THINK** about how might the therapist work with clients with learning disabilities to enable them to use the model.

# Chapter 6: Trauma and Its impact on Relationships – the work of Wilfred Bion and David Malan

## The work of Wilfred Bion

Bion was an American psychologist who did a lot of work with veterans from the First and Second World Wars. He is famous for the work he did with groups of soldiers which has greatly increased our understanding of groups more widely.

In this chapter we are most interested in the work he did with people who had suffered very traumatic experiences in the wars. These people were suffering from what at the time was called 'shell shock'. We now know this as 'post traumatic stress disorder' (PTSD). He noticed that when a person had been severely traumatised their personality became 'disintegrated'. It was almost as if the person's personality had become 'lost'.

## 'Attacks on linking'

While doing therapeutic work with these very traumatised people, Bion noticed that sometimes he found himself feeling very sleepy or almost mesmerised by the person he was with. Because of this he found that it was very difficult to think about what the person was saying and that he was unable to make 'links' or connections between what they were bringing to the sessions. Bion realised that what was happening was very important and called this process *'attacks on linking'*. He discovered that this is an unconscious process which can interfere with the ability to think properly when with a very traumatised person. This happens because the person's trauma is so overwhelming it would be too much for them to be able to see the links and connections between what has happened to them. Bion realised that the person's personality being disintegrated is actually a way of the mind coping with the awful trauma. The unconscious tries to maintain the chaos that is happening in the person's internal world to stop any links from being made as these would be too overwhelming.

# How this applies to people with disabilities

We now know that people with disabilities can also be very traumatised. This occurs either from the experience of their disability, their early life experiences or later traumas. It can also be due to a combination of all these things.

Being with someone in this condition can make you feel overwhelmed with tiredness or that you are not able to think properly. You may feel mesmerised by the person or very sleepy. This is a very frightening thing for staff to feel. They may worry that they are not doing their job properly or are not being professional. Therefore, it is important to be aware of this process and understand why it is happening.

Having this kind of experience with someone indicates that the person has had a trauma that is too painful to be faced. They may actually appear on the surface to be OK and happy. However, if the person has this mesmerising effect on people they may need to be referred to a therapist for help and support.

 **STOP AND THINK** about whether you have ever had this experience with someone you have supported in the past. Think about whether what you have just read helps you to make sense of this experience.

## Therapeutic work with these people

Working therapeutically with people with PTSD or other deep trauma is very specialised work. If the therapist finds themselves being affected they need to think about what was so difficult in the session that it couldn't be faced or tolerated. If the person couldn't look at it, their unconscious has attacked any links the therapist tried to make so that they couldn't look at it either.

If a therapist has this experience they will need to discuss it with a colleague or supervisor. By doing this they can think about what it might be in the person's life that can't be faced. They can then go into future sessions being mindful of what might be happening and what the person might not be able to bear.

Gradually, by the therapist themselves being aware of the issue, it is able to be faced, initially by the therapist and then by the client. This process will not happen in one session and will take time.

# Linking the present to the past – ideas from David Malan

David Malan was a one of a later generation of psychotherapists. In his book, *Psychodynamic Psychotherapy and the Science of Psychodynamics* (1979), Malan brought together all the ideas of psychodynamic working that had been developed by earlier psychotherapists. He described what happens in one-to-one therapy and developed a model that can be used to measure the effectiveness of therapy.

Malan stressed that we all become who we are through our experiences. Part of being a human being is having had both good and difficult experiences. Sometimes we may be frightened of these difficult experiences or not want to think about them and therefore they may be hidden away from consciousness. However, if we can tolerate, understand and analyse what has happened to us and how we have been affected, then it is possible to have a better quality of life.

Malan outlined a number of principles that are essential to psychotherapy:

- the therapist having unconditional acceptance of the client
- a relationship being established between the client and therapist and rapport being built up between them
- that the aim of psychotherapy is to enable to client to understand their feelings, bring them closer to consciousness and experience them.

To do this, Malan said it was necessary for the therapist to make judgements about five areas:

1. The degree to which the client is already in touch with their true feelings.
2. The nature of the hidden feelings that the client is not yet aware of.
3. How accessible those feelings are.
4. The degree of anxiety that is likely to be associated with those feelings.
5. The client's capacity to bear this anxiety.

The model Malan developed to show what happens in therapy is called *Malan's Triangles*.

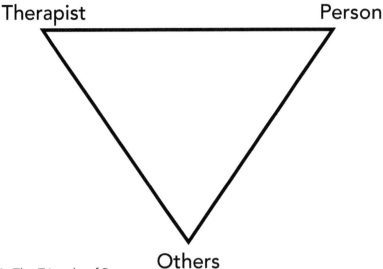

**Figure 6.1:** The Triangle of Person

This triangle is made up of the person (or client), the therapist and others. 'Others' means other people in the client's life, either in the present or in the past.

In therapy the relationship is between the client and the therapist. However, what is brought to therapy, to be helped with, is feelings from the relationship between the client and other people, usually people from their past. These may be deeply buried or the person is not aware of them and this is why they are at the bottom of the triangle.

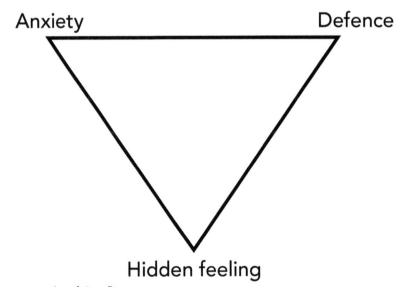

**Figure 6.2:** Triangle of Conflict

This second triangle contains the client's anxiety, defence and their hidden feelings. The hidden feelings relate to the others from the client's past and because they are hidden they are not in the person's awareness, which is why they are at the bottom of the triangle. When the client comes to the sessions with the therapist they are 'defended'. This means that they are unconsciously using a defence against the anxiety that relates to the hidden feelings. The client will not be aware of these defences at this stage.

 **STOP AND THINK** Can you think of examples which may fit within Malan's Triangle of Person, and Triangle of Conflict?

# What happens in therapy

In therapy, the person/client will talk about people and experiences from their past but in a defended way. A common example is that people will say they had a really happy childhood, when actually things happened that have caused them difficulties in their present life. This statement defends against the anxiety that the therapist will see the hidden feelings they have about their childhood and people in their past.

It is important to remember that the feelings are hidden from the client as well. The person is using defences to protect themselves from the pain of these hidden feelings. The hidden feelings are usually about people from the past. This is most usually the parents, but can be anybody.

The process of therapy is to gradually bring the hidden feelings and the person's relationship with others into the relationship between the client and the therapist. By doing this the anxiety can be faced without having to defend against it. In this way the hidden feelings and the relationships with the other people can be explored and come to terms with.

In his book, Malan says that the therapist and client need to progress through nine different stages.

The first stage is that the person can tolerate being in the room with the therapist. The second stage is they can talk about the fact that there might be something in their past that is interfering with their present. This process goes on until the hidden feelings are faced.

At this point the person has reached a point known as 'assimilation'. This means that the person has processed the issues from the past and no longer has to defend against them. The difficult hidden feelings can now be tolerated.

People vary in how long it takes them to get to this point. Some people may do it very quickly while others may need a couple of years to get there. How long it takes depends on how defended the person is about the past and how intense the hidden feelings are.

Malan wrote (1979):

> *'The aim of most dynamic psychotherapy is to reach beneath the defence and the anxiety to the hidden feeling and then to trace this feeling back from the present to its origins in the past, usually in relation to the parents.'*

The process of doing this is particularly delicate and needs to be done very carefully by a skilled therapist.

# People with learning disabilities

There has been some work done using these ideas and models with people with learning disabilities. This works shows that people can still use the model. They may not get to the full stage of assimilation, but people do make enough progress in the model that they are able to let issues from the past come into consciousness so they can work with them.

The therapist may need to work in more creative ways with people with learning disabilities as they may not be able to talk about their life in the way that non-disabled people do. The therapist will need to think more about a person's behaviour and also their own feelings in the sessions to help the person progress through the stages of therapy.

 **STOP AND THINK** – How might the therapist work with clients with learning disabilities to enable them to use the model?

# Chapter 7: Disability Issues Understood from Valerie Sinason

Valerie Sinason was a pioneer in working with people with learning disabilities using psychotherapy. She started out her career as an English teacher but later trained as a psychotherapist. She worked at the Tavistock Clinic in London, which is a national centre for psychotherapy.

In the 1980s and early 1990s, Sinason formed a group with some of her colleagues. They began using psychotherapy with people with learning disabilities. The group supported and supervised each other in this work. They began to see some very positive changes in the people they worked with.

Sinason wrote about this work in her book *Mental Handicap and the Human Condition*, which was published in 1992. This book was one of the first to show that people with learning disabilities can benefit from psychotherapy. The book includes case studies and text from actual sessions with people. It is extremely interesting reading and gives an insight into what happens in therapy sessions; in it, Sinason introduced a number of new ideas and concepts from her work. This chapter will cover some of these. Firstly, however, it is important to understand how things were for people with learning disabilities before Sinason started her work.

## How things were before Sinason

Up until the 1980s it was usually thought that people with learning disabilities were not affected by emotional events. It was felt that because of their disability they couldn't understand upsetting things and therefore would not be distressed by them. If a person with learning disabilities did show any distress or difficult behaviours it was seen as being part of their condition, or their learning disability, rather than anything else. The most common treatments for people were either medication or behavioural approaches. Medication was usually anti-psychotics or heavy tranquilisers. These either sedated the person or knocked them out, and were known as the 'chemical cosh'.

Behavioural approaches at this time were not as sophisticated as they are now. They worked on rewarding appropriate behaviour and either ignoring or punishing inappropriate behaviours. Therefore, someone's distressed behaviour would often either be ignored or punished.

We now know that people with learning disabilities do suffer from emotional distress. Up to 40 per cent of people with a learning disability will suffer a mental illness at some point in their lives. This is almost double the rate of the general population.

Today, treatments are much better. Behavioural approaches look at why the person is behaving the way they are and what they are gaining from it. Support then helps the person to get their needs met in better ways. People may also have access to talking therapies. However, even with these improvements, there is still often a lack of understanding of the emotional lives of people with learning disabilities.

Valerie Sinason's work has helped to change this and has contributed to the development of disability psychotherapy. Before her work, it was generally felt that people with learning disabilities were also not intelligent enough to benefit from psychotherapy. The reason for this is because psychotherapy is about talking about a person's life, their past and things that have happened to them and then making sense of how this affects them in their present lives. Because of their learning disability, people may struggle with memory, with expressing themselves verbally or be confused about things. Because of this it was felt that they wouldn't be able to benefit from psychotherapy.

There had been some earlier attempts to use psychotherapy with people with learning disabilities. In 1933 Clark published the successful work he had started with people with learning disabilities. Unfortunately, his worked was stopped by the Second World War and not picked up again. Sinason's work has shown again that people can benefit greatly from psychotherapy. She has been a major driving force in the current development of the approach.

# The pain of difference

For Sinason, this was a key issue; she described the emotional pain that people with disabilities often feel by being different from non-disabled people. No matter how small a difference between oneself and a non-disabled person, it is very difficult to deal with the emotional pain of this. Sinason pointed out that it may be easier for the person to exaggerate the handicap rather than come to terms with the difference. This often results in the person's intelligence being masked and their potential restricted.

Frankish, P. (2021). *Trauma-informed Care in Intellectual Disability.* © Pavilion Publishing and Media Ltd.

Sinason felt it important to highlight this pain of difference because society prefers not to acknowledge it. This is because it is very difficult to bear thinking about people being in so much pain. In the past, society has dealt with it by denying that people experience this pain by thinking that learning disabled people are unfeeling beings.

# 'Secondary handicap'

Sinason realised that many of the distressed people she was seeing had what she called a 'secondary handicap', in addition to the disability they are born with. Sinason describes how:

> *'...the defensive use or abuse the individual makes of primary damage can sometimes be more powerful than the original handicap itself.'*

Secondary handicap is a reaction to the emotional issues and distress the person carries and can actually cause their learning disability to become worse. This causes another layer of difficulty for the person to deal with and prevents them from reaching their full potential.

When thinking about secondary handicap, it is important to remember that disability is the thing that the person is born with, or develops in life, that 'handicaps' them. The handicap makes it harder to do or achieve things in life. Therefore, a secondary handicap is something in addition to the disability they were born with, and that further handicaps them.

A secondary handicap may show itself in a number of different ways, including the person's intellectual skills being poorer than would be expected from the disability they were born with. Other types of secondary handicap may be a person being self-injurious or violent towards themselves. A person may also be aggressive to other people. Or they may show inappropriate sexual behaviours which make them vulnerable.

The way a secondary handicap presents itself often indicates the trauma a person has experienced i.e. if they have experienced violence, they may injure themselves or if they have been sexually abused they may show inappropriate sexual behaviours.

**STOP AND THINK** about secondary handicap. Read the poem below and think about what it means. You may need to read it through a few times.

# Head banger

'The man kicked the telly right

so he smashed smashed

with his great fists

at the stubborn interference

in his brain.

His knuckles grew lumps

his forehead grew bumps

but the picture did not change.

'Birdbrain' cries his mother

feeding him plaster and flannels

helmets and hugs.

She could see

it was an injured eagle

that flickered

in the half light of his eyes

that would never be right

and when he let his eyes

open wide

he kicked the television

to pieces.'

In this poem, Sinason writes about the pain that people carry about their disability and how a secondary handicap may present itself. In the poem the man shows violence towards himself. He is doing this to try and correct the 'disturbance' in his brain. The reason for this is because he has seen someone fixing the disturbance on a television by hitting it. There is also a sense that the man has been doing this to himself for a long time. This is an example of a secondary handicap that is occurring because of the pain he feels at being disabled and having disturbance in his brain.

This violence to himself and also to the television at the end of the poem is handicapping him further and stunting his potential, more than the disability he was born with. If this man was given the opportunity to process his emotional pain about his disability, he may be able to stop some of the aggression he is showing to himself and things around him.

## Three types of secondary handicap

In her book Sinason talks about three types of secondary handicap. These are now discussed in more detail below. These three types may exist together.

### Mild secondary handicap

One of the very difficult facts to think about regarding people with disabilities is that sometimes they are completely dependent on those around them. They need carers for day-to-day support and sometimes even their very survival to provide food, shelter and safety.

Because of this very difficult fact, Sinason said that some people may present themselves in such a way that they 'put on a front', to please and not upset those caring for them. They do this to keep those carers happy and to ensure they keep supporting them. But to do this means having to suppress, or 'push down', any emotional pain and distress they may be feeling because showing it may upset those who are caring for them.

> *'It's as though people think that they have enough to deal with just with the very presence of a disabled person, without having to deal with any kind of distress or unhappiness as well'.*

The person may do this unconsciously and not be aware of what they are doing. This is similar to Winnicott's ideas about how the false self develops by the child fitting in with what the carer wants and suppressing its own true needs and feelings.

The person then has to keep all their pain and anger inside and not express it. This suppresses the person's already damaged intellectual abilities because of the energy needed to do this. They then become more disabled than they were.

 **STOP AND THINK** about times in your life when you have been stressed or distressed. Did you notice how this made it more difficult for you to think clearly or remember things? For someone who is distressed this is what can happen to their intellectual abilities. Now think about how it would have felt trying to hide those feelings of distress or upset you had – indeed you may have done this. For someone who is experiencing mild secondary handicap by trying to hide their pain and distress, this is a permanent state.

Sinason talked about the *'handicapped smile'* seen by a person trying always to look happy, by smiling no matter how they are feeling. The handicapped smile is really there to protect those around the person from seeing their pain and distress.

*'Someone afflicted with mental and physical pain has less reason to smile and feel happy than the rest of the population and yet there is tremendous pressure to insist on signs of pleasure precisely because of that.'*

By this she means that because as a society we struggle to accept and deal with the pain and distress that people often feel, there is pressure on those people to hide their pain and distress. But this means the disabled person then has more problems to deal with.

Only when the person can express their feelings and come to terms with their disability can they try to resume a normal life, with true happiness rather than pretences. If this is not allowed to happen, a person's potential will always be restricted.

## Opportunist handicap

Another type of secondary handicap that Sinason talks about is the 'opportunist handicap'. This refers to the accumulated emotional distress caused over a lifetime by having a disability.

If we think back to the ideas of Winnicott and Bowlby, they stressed that the experiences in the first few years of life are the building blocks for later robust mental health. We have seen in this text how these early years, the primary care relationship and attachment can be affected by the disability. This leads the person to be more vulnerable to poor mental health in later life. They may also be at more risk of being exploited and traumatised. They may have difficult behaviours or poor relationships with others. Because the person's emotional robustness is not as strong, they will be more vulnerable to the psychological impact of any further difficulties in later life.

Sinason's term 'opportunist handicap' refers to the build-up, over a lifetime of all the emotional disturbance caused by the disability. The distress that this accumulation causes can lead to the person being more handicapped than they were by the disability they were born with.

## Secondary handicap as a defence

The third type of secondary handicap that Sinason talked about was when it is used as a 'defence' against trauma. A 'defence' is a psychological mechanism that serves to block out emotional pain, so it is not felt. This is often unconscious, meaning we are not even aware of it. Denial is a very common defence where emotional pain is 'pushed down' out of conscious awareness so we don't have to think about it.

In this type of secondary handicap the person is protecting themselves from some trauma they have experienced which is in addition to being disabled. Unfortunately, people with disabilities are much more vulnerable to suffering life traumas. Statistics show that people with learning disabilities are much more vulnerable to sexual abuse or assault, physical and verbal abuse than the rest of the population. It is also common for people with learning disabilities to experience a great deal of loss.

The case study below, taken from Sinason's book, highlights this type of secondary handicap in a young girl who has been sexually abused.

## Maria

Maria is a five-year-old girl with learning difficulties. Once she was able to express more of her experience of abuse, more of her intelligence returned to her. In one session she tore the head off the 'father doll'.

*'Stupid daddy, I've thrown his head away. Now he is only a body. He can't see, hear or know. He doesn't know what I am doing to him because he has not got a mind'.*

She threw him across the room and laughed angrily and then did the same with the 'mother doll'. She wanted me and her parents to know what she had felt like, deprived of her head, her sight, her intellect. Maria, however, did not have learning disabilities. It was easy to see that her learning difficulties had an emotional base.

Sinason attempts to explain why this type of secondary handicap is such a common occurrence, why people find it so much easier to try and ignore their abuse and hide behind a pretence of misunderstanding, and in a sense, 'stupidity' – meaning a state of unawareness or stupefication. She says:

*'If surviving means cutting your head off, your intellect is destroyed. If knowing and seeing involves knowing and seeing terrible things, it is not surprising that not knowing, becoming stupid, becomes a defence.'*

This means that the person is less able to think about the trauma or loss they have experienced and in this way they are able to carry on. However, the cost of this to the person is that their learning disability worsens and their cognitive skills decrease, making life much more difficult for them.

### The sense in 'stupidity'

Sinason describes how the word 'stupid', which is commonly used as an insult or derogatory term, actually comes from the word 'stupefy', which means 'numbed with grief'. It this context it makes sense that someone may exaggerate their handicap/disability and retreat into their own world, rather than have to come to terms with the pain and distress of their experiences.

This is especially so when the person has to deal with the traumatic experience on their own, without help. In this way it makes sense that a person would retreat into their own world as a way to avoid pain and distress.

# Cognitive and emotional intelligence

Through her work, Sinason has disproved the belief that people have to be 'intelligent enough' to benefit from psychotherapy. She worked with people who had a whole range of learning disabilities, from mild to profound. In her book she shares the intense and moving changes made by the people she worked with. Sinason showed that someone doesn't have to have a certain level of cognitive intelligence to benefit from psychotherapy, as was previously thought. She highlighted that someone with reduced cognitive or intellectual intelligence can still have great 'emotional intelligence' and this is the important factor in being able to benefit from psychotherapy.

> *'However crippled someone's external functional intelligence might be, there can still be intact a complex emotional structure and capacity.'*

Sinason cites an example by Stokes (1987) involving a 24-year-old woman who has Downs syndrome describing her feelings about her birth:

> *'I just wanted to be inside my mummy's tummy again. I wondered what was the point of coming out – I am pushed around on the underground and they make me feel small. I think it was nice in there. I was thinking why was I born and why did my mother bring me up like this.'*

This shows the amount of emotional intelligence the woman had in describing her feelings about being born, even though on measures of cognitive intelligence she did not perform highly.

One of the most important features of psychotherapy is enabling the person to express their emotions and tell their story. The way therapy is done with the person may need to be modified to help them overcome the difficulties they may

Frankish, P. (2021). *Trauma-informed Care in Intellectual Disability.* © Pavilion Publishing and Media Ltd.

have, such as with communication. This may be done using drawing, drama or creative activities. The therapy needs to be modified according to the specific needs of the person.

## Impact of therapy

Sinason found that by helping a person process their pain and distress rather than blocking it out or showing it in difficult behaviours, the person's secondary handicap reduced.

What Sinason and other therapists often see when working with people in this way, is that a person's difficult behaviours may stop or reduce. Once people have begun to trust the therapist and are established in therapy, their language abilities may increase. Often, a person's cognitive abilities will also improve over the course of the therapy.

These are all examples of the person 'letting go' of their secondary handicap. They no longer need it to protect them as they have processed their emotional pain. What has happened to them, although still traumatic and difficult, is tolerable to the extent they do not have to block it out. They no longer have the additional problems a secondary handicap can cause and can begin to live their lives and move towards reaching their potential.

It is important to stress that this is not the removal or 'cure' of the person's learning disability. It is the removal of the secondary handicap which was adding to their difficulties. By reducing the secondary handicap, a person can function at the level they were before their emotional distress or trauma.

## Summary

Valerie Sinason introduces some topics and issues that are very hard to think about. She makes us consider the way that people with learning disabilities are treated in our society which can often lead to their disabilities becoming more severe. People may be traumatised, but in subtle ways are discouraged from showing their emotional pain as it is too difficult for those around them to bear.

Sinason has also showed us very clearly that if we can stop denying this pain and trauma and admit it exists, we can then begin to help people process their distress. They will gain not only emotional relief, but can also begin to let go of the secondary handicap which they have been using to protect themselves.

The person can move towards having a happier, more fulfilled life, with more chance to reach their full potential. They may be able to become more independent with a more robust sense of self and maybe even need less support.

# Chapter 8: Observations and Interventions – Using the FAIT

## Introduction

In this chapter we look again at the work of Margaret Mahler and her colleagues in developing a structure through which to observe and understand emotional development in young children. The Frankish Assessment of the Impact of Trauma in Intellectual Disability (FAIT) tool is useful in undertaking that assessment and enabling an effective series of interventions. In this chapter, we look again at the behaviours informing each stage of development, and go on to detail how to map this behaviour using the FAIT tool.

## Making an assessment

In order to establish the emotional developmental stage of the distressed individual it is necessary to carry out an observation, based on the theory of Margaret Mahler, as described in Chapter 3. The time needed has been established through research, and 40 minutes is sufficient. It takes a bit of practice to learn to do it but most people can become proficient after two or three attempts.

- Decide on a person who you will be able to watch for 40 minutes.
- Observe the person for 20 seconds
- Use the next 40 seconds to write exactly what you observed.
- Continue in this way until the full 40 minutes have been completed.
- Rate each of your observation points (each 20 seconds) based on Mahler's theory.

# Mapping the stages to the FAIT

## Symbiotic stage

The *symbiotic stage* is the newborn phase in the first few weeks of life. At this stage it is as if the mother and child are still connected. This is the stage that Winnicott described, when the mother and child are in a very close enmeshed relationship.

This is called the *symbiotic relationship*. In the symbiotic stage the child is entirely dependent on the mother to have all its needs met. **This is rarely seen and not included in the FAIT**.

## Differentiation stage

The differentiation stage is when the baby develops an awareness of itself and the parts of its body. This stage starts at a few weeks and goes to about nine months. At this stage babies will look at and play with their hands, feet and sometimes their genitals. They also become aware of their immediate surroundings such as the cot or pram that they are in and the toys that are around them. At this stage the baby is only aware of a very small space around it and is beginning to notice that it exists within this small space.

All of the behaviours seen in the differentiation stage are called 'self-referenced behaviours'. This means that everything the baby does is about, or in reference to, itself. It doesn't do anything to influence anybody else. Although if the baby screams or cries this will influences others; the reason the baby does it, is because it wants something for itself i.e. is hungry or cold. The baby therefore is only aware of other people being around in terms of getting its own needs met.
**This is rated 1 in the FAIT**.

## Practising stage

Brain development in babies happens very quickly. Through this rapid brain development the baby becomes able to do new things on a very regular basis. Mahler found that the baby will start to 'practise' a new skill as it becomes available. The baby will practise the new skill again and again until it can do it well.

Examples of this would be the baby throwing the rattle out of the pram and doing so again and again. Other behaviours would be learning to roll over, crawling and standing up.

This stage begins at around nine months and continues to around 15 months. The baby may practise behaviours at other times but this is the main practising stage.

When the child can do a particular behaviour well, another becomes available due to the brain's rapid development. The child then begins practising this new behaviour.

It is very important in the practising stage that someone is around watching and paying attention to the child. Mahler found that if the child knew it was being watched, then the practising behaviour continued. If the child thought that nobody was paying attention they practiced much less. This would make learning a new behaviour much slower. **This is rated 2 in the FAIT.**

## Rapprochement stage

The word rapprochement means *'give and take'*. Give and take is one of the most important skills needed in relationships. In this stage the child is beginning to have a two-way, or reciprocal, relationship with its primary carers. This stage is divided into two sub-stages – early rapprochement and late rapprochement. It goes from about 15 months to about three and a half years.

### Early rapprochement

The early rapprochement stage is the start of the child beginning to learn to give and take. This begins around 15 months and goes on until about two years. The first sign that a child has moved into the early rapprochement stage is when the child begins to say 'no', or walks away. This shows the start of two-way negotiation.

The child moving into this stage can be challenging for the parents. It is sometimes called the 'terrible twos'. In this stage the child will become interested in 'peek-a-boo' or 'round and round the garden' games, which are about two-way communication and give and take between two people. **This is rated 3 in the FAIT.**

### Late rapprochement

The late rapprochement stage is the beginning of the child moving towards independence. This stage can be more challenging as the child is negotiating and can be demanding in getting its needs met. This happens from two to three years.

In this stage the child also gradually begins to increase the distance it can be away from the primary carers or parents. It can do this with its levels of anxiety being manageable. This is similar to the ideas of Winnicott (1964) and Bowlby (1988), who talked about the child gradually having the confidence to move away from the mother, or 'safe base', and explore the world.

It is really important that the child's anxiety is manageable so they are not overwhelmed. Independence grows in small steps that the child can cope with. For example, at play group the child may start off being sat by its mother's feet. When it is a few months older the child will move away to play with the other children in the middle of the floor. It can do this by being able to keep an eye on mum and where she is. As the child moves into late rapprochement, it will be able to go a bit further away from mum. It can do this without being anxious about where she is.

*'Emotional refuelling'* is important in this stage to help the child feel confident. This is where the child will look round for the parent and make eye contact. This eye contact will 'emotionally refuel' the child and help them feel confident. They can then happily carry on playing at a distance from the carer.

By having the confidence to move away from the carer the child can begin to explore. Through this the child is learning about the world around it. The child is also beginning to understand its own place in the world. **This is rated 4 in the FAIT**.

## Individuation stage

Once the child has moved fairly smoothly through the stages above it reaches the individuation stage. This is the point where the child can be separate from the primary carer with manageable anxiety. Note this is not a state of having no anxiety. It is normal and indeed sometimes helpful to have some manageable anxiety. It is a state of not being overwhelmed by anxiety when separated from the parent or primary carer.

Some children reach the individuation stage through a 'rapprochement crisis'. This is when they realise the primary carer is not there, they become anxious, distressed and may have a tantrum. They then realise that they can cope with the situation.

Individuation is the point of the child knowing that they are separate from the carer but that they can manage the anxiety of this. Reaching the individuation stage is the 'psychological birth' of the child. It is the point that they have reached their own identity, as being separate from their parents.

At this point the child is psychologically able to grow further into an independent human being who can stand on their own two feet. **This is not rated in the FAIT as people who are individuated would be unlikely to be referred**.

*All of this is described in the FAIT (Frankish Assessment of the Impact of Trauma).*

# Mapping the assessment to interventions

From the observations it is possible to establish a child's emotional developmental stage. This is then linked to the cognitive stage and the physical age to establish the level of desynchrony for the individual. This will usually give a fairly clear understanding of the meaning of the distressed behaviour.

## Deepak

Deepak is a 30-year-old man who is cognitively functioning at about age eight but is emotionally measured at age 18 months. He will be struggling to maintain or establish a sense of self because of the confusing messages he will be receiving. Some people will expect him to behave like a 30-year-old, some will make allowances for his cognitive impairment but few will realise that inside he is a toddler trying to get looked after.

On the following page you will find an *Observation sheet* template, which you are free to photocopy. Alternatively you can download and print a PDF or Word document from www.pavpub.com/fait-resources.

It is a simple chart, which you can easily draw up yourself, if needs be, writing numbers 1 to 40 on a sheet of paper, and then the observations alongside.

# Observation sheet

Please record the details of the 40-minute observation in the table below. For each 20 seconds you have observed, write what you have seen for 40 seconds and then repeat this so you have a total of 40 observations. When you have finished the 40 observations, review your notes and grade each observation by ticking the relevant box using the following key:

**1** = Differentiation          **2** = Practising
**3** = Early rapprochement      **4** = Late rapprochement

| | Description of what you have seen | Grade 1 | 2 | 3 | 4 |
|---|---|---|---|---|---|
| 1 | | | | | |
| 2 | | | | | |
| 3 | | | | | |
| 4 | | | | | |
| 5 | | | | | |
| 6 | | | | | |
| 7 | | | | | |
| 8 | | | | | |
| 9 | | | | | |
| 10 | | | | | |
| 11 | | | | | |
| 12 | | | | | |
| 13 | | | | | |
| 14 | | | | | |
| 15 | | | | | |
| 16 | | | | | |
| 17 | | | | | |
| 18 | | | | | |
| 19 | | | | | |

| | Description of what you have seen | Grade | | | |
|---|---|---|---|---|---|
| | | 1 | 2 | 3 | 4 |
| 20 | | | | | |
| 21 | | | | | |
| 22 | | | | | |
| 23 | | | | | |
| 24 | | | | | |
| 25 | | | | | |
| 26 | | | | | |
| 27 | | | | | |
| 28 | | | | | |
| 29 | | | | | |
| 30 | | | | | |
| 31 | | | | | |
| 32 | | | | | |
| 33 | | | | | |
| 34 | | | | | |
| 35 | | | | | |
| 36 | | | | | |
| 37 | | | | | |
| 38 | | | | | |
| 39 | | | | | |
| 40 | | | | | |
| | **Total** | | | | |

# Interventions

## General

Most people referred will be very distressed. They will have an intellectual disability and additional issues. If they 'just' had the disability, they would usually have progressed through special schooling and into adult life with relatively few difficulties. A disability is not automatically associated with behavioural problems or mental health issues. There must be another component. That component is trauma. The cause of the traumatic response will be very individual. What is traumatising for one person is not necessarily traumatising for another. Identifying the stage of arrested emotional development gives the signpost for the traumatic event. The way it is expressed gives further information. So the person who attacks themselves will have had a different experience from the person who attacks others.

Once the assessment is completed and the type and age of the trauma is known it becomes possible to plan an intervention. Anyone who is traumatised before the stage of individuation will need a 'significant other' available at all times. For those at the differentiation, practising and early rapprochement stages, this needs to be someone who can work with them on a one-to-one basis. Once they have progressed to late rapprochement they can begin to share and accept that their person is available but may not be visible all the time. There are times when the staffing level needs to start with more than one person present but, if providing the right support, it reduces after a time. Even if it takes a few years for a 20-year-old who will potentially live to be 70 or 80, helping them to grow and achieve a sense of self and enabling them to live an ordinary life is 'worth the investment', in every way.

Some people harm themselves and others to such an extent that they may be in services where they are restrained, perhaps by up to six or seven people. This is in itself traumatising. They are better with a safe room, soft lined and low stimulus, perhaps with soothing music to go to until calm. The support staff can stay in verbal communication through the door and be ready to support the person as soon as they are able to come out. This requires that the staff are always supportive and not punitive, clearly trying to help and understand, not punish the distressed behaviour. Staff training and support is vital for this to work. There is a danger that the staff are reinforced by the absence of the individual and this must not be allowed to happen. There have been some very sad cases of individuals shut in safe rooms all the time, with some of them dying young as a consequence. Careful management of safe-rooms is vital.

# Designing stage-specific interventions and practice

## Differentiation stage

The specific interventions to address the stage of development will be built on the known factors. The person who is at the differentiation level must not be asked for anything. All must be given freely, unconditionally and with no expectation of thanks or response. Once this is trusted to happen, the person will relax and start to look forward to staff approaching. Smiling and communication is likely to follow. Initially, for very withdrawn people, it is worth setting up a timed programme for approaching, recording the response. If it is on a set pattern, the person will soon start to look for you coming. This is equivalent to working with a baby of less than one year old. However, the cognitive ability is likely to be higher so needs to be recognised with the type of activities, clothes, equipment, language and such like, pitched at the cognitive level. Once the relationship is established the person will start to do more things and take an interest. This is the beginning of *practising*.

## Practising stage

This stage involves lots of repetitive behaviours. They are often seen as autistic, which they may be. But not all autistic people are traumatised (as far as we know) and certainly they don't all express distressed behaviour. The practising stage is equivalent to approximately 10 to 15 months, so a time of exploration. Saying out loud what is happening is helpful, so when out walking, draw attention to the surroundings, where walking and such like. Try to develop an interest in the world and develop skills – lots of simple activities that are done for the sake of doing them, not necessarily for the result. Always be 'in front' – that is, planning what is next, so as to avoid confrontation. Starting the day with, 'We're going to get up, showered and have breakfast' gives a steer. Then, before breakfast is finished, 'We'll tidy up next and then find our shoes to go out'. It keeps the concentration on activity and avoids confrontation or interpersonal pressure and expectations.

## Early rapprochement

For people who are established in the practising stage it is time to start some early rapprochement activities. These are two-way interactions. Games are a good place to start, like Connect 4 or draughts. Card games are also good, as are sharing tasks such as setting the table, putting things away in turns, anything that involves working or playing with another person. Most staff find this the easiest stage as there is usually lots to get involved with and a sense of working together. It does usually involve more interesting things to do as it is usually safe to go out in the community more, knowing that there will be a response if needed. This is the equivalent of the stage that leads up to the challenges of the 'terrible twos'. Some staff would prefer that the people they support stay in this stage as the next one is more demanding. However, it is important to keep on trying to enable the supported person to develop further. A lot of behaviour at this stage is designed to communicate, so needs to be observed for the consequences, which will facilitate the identification of the meaning. There is some willingness to respond to reward programmes at this stage.

## Late rapprochement

This is the last stage before individuation and involves lots of challenges, negotiations, jostling for position, attempts at independence. The role of support staff is to encourage these developments, while making sure that safety considerations are not forgotten, that the range of activities is wide and varied, and that attempts at social development become more important. There are tantrums in this stage and a lot of 'it's not fair'. Staff need a lot of support to stay focused during this stage. It lasts quite a long time, maybe up to two years, but getting to the end of it provides a much better future for the individual. They can be more independent, more able to make rational choices and just be generally more adult emotionally. The level of intellectual disability won't fundamentally change but the ability that is there becomes more accessible to the individual. Some people have shown increase in IQ score on tests after reaching a more mature emotional level, but this isn't usually the aim, just a useful addition.

Individuals in the late rapprochement stage should be able to benefit from *positive behaviour support* as the degree of 'working together' increases. They become more able to bargain, agree on what is fair, and choose between options. They become much more able to work for delayed gratification rewards at this stage.

## Individuation

It is more difficult for someone to fully individuate if their intellectual disability means they cannot be fully independent. However, they can reach a stage of being able to express their views and choices, and to negotiate to get what they want. It is important to recognise when there is maturity in negotiation and accept that, working with the person to help them achieve their goals. This is different from the early rapprochement demands and care needs to be taken to identify the correct stage.

Frankish, P. (2021). *Trauma-informed Care in Intellectual Disability.* © Pavilion Publishing and Media Ltd.

## A note of caution

Most staff find it hard to accept that grown people are emotionally less than three years old and will understandably allocate a higher level than is appropriate. Doing the observation carefully, to check, is the best way forward or, sometimes, to ask someone else who doesn't know the individual. If the wrong stage is allocated there will be a deterioration in behaviour. Being in tune with the person is the crucial factor and that only comes from knowing what you are tuning in to.

# Management of safe rooms

A safe room should be just that – safe. It should not be a seclusion room that shuts away the problem. Its main purpose is to avoid the use of restraint, which is traumatising because it involves overpowering another human being. When it is decided that a safe room is needed, the individual care plans must reflect the issues for that person. The criteria for using the room must be risk of harm to self or others. Big cushions can be used to guide the person to the room, to avoid any hands-on trauma. The door needs to be a three-quarters door, with space at top to communicate through. If the distressed person is saying 'go away' then staff need to withdraw and return on a schedule of timings to check that all is OK, say every 10 minutes. When the individual is ready to communicate they can be offered a drink and gradually returned to the main living space. I have seen some safe-rooms misused and become the main living space. This must not be allowed to happen as it is a backward step, leading to more withdrawal and deterioration in emotional stage, not progress.

# Footnote

The identification of the right stage is essential for working out appropriate care plans and day-to-day living experiences that will be therapeutic.

Additional individual therapy will involve considering all the other theories put forward here, to identify what is relevant to the individual person's history and what has been traumatic for them. Direct support staff can support the individual therapy through understanding, and tolerating, the pain with them.

# References and recommended reading

Bowlby J (1999) [1969] Attachment. Attachment and Loss (vol. 1) (2nd edn). New York: Basic Books.

Bowlby J (1973) Separation: Anxiety & Anger. Attachment and Loss (vol. 2); (International psycho-analytical library no.95). London: Hogarth Press.

Bowlby J (1980) Loss: Sadness & Depression. Attachment and Loss (vol. 3); (International psycho-analytical library no.109). London: Hogarth Press.

Bowlby J (1988) A Secure Base: Parent-Child Attachment and Healthy Human Development. London: Routledge. *This book combines Bowlby's most well-known books about attachment into one book. This will give a good detailed understanding of how attachment and the safe base is important at all stages of life.*

Clark P (1933) *The Nature and Treatment of Amentia*. London: Balliere.

Frankish P (1989) Meeting the emotional needs of handicapped people: a psychodynamic approach. Journal of Mental Deficiency Research 33 407–414.

Frankish P (1992) A psychodynamic approach to emotional difficulties within a social framework. *Journal of Intellectual Disability Research* **36** 559–563.

Frankish P (2015) *Disability Psychotherapy: An innovative approach to trauma-informed care.* London: Karnac Books.

Freud S (1927) *The Ego and the ID. (The International Psycho-Analytic Library, No.12).* London: Hogarth Press.

Gerhardt S (2004) *Why Love Matters: How affection shapes a baby's brain.* London: Routledge. *This book gives an overview of the biological and neurological evidence that science now finds supports the work of Bowlby and Winnicott.*

Klein M (1998) *The Collected Writings of Melanie Klein (Volumes 1–4).* London: Hogarth Press.

Malan DH (1979) *Psychodynamic Psychotherapy and the Science of Psychodynamics.* London: Butterworth-Heinemann.

Mahler S, Pine F and Bergman A (1975) *The Psychological Birth of the Human Infant: Symbiosis and individuation.* New York: Basic Books.

Rodman R and Winnicott DW (1971) *Playing and Reality.* London: Tavistock. *This book discusses the importance of play in a child's development.*

Sinason V (1992) *Mental Handicap and the Human Condition: New Approaches from the Tavistock.* London: Free Association Books.

Stokes J (1987) *Insights form psychotherapy.* Paper presented at International Symposium on Mental Handicap, Royal Society of medicine 25 February.

Winnicott DW (1964) *The Child, The Family and the Outside World.* London: Pelican Books. *This is a very easy-to-read book that gives a really good insight into Winnicott's ideas about the early years of a child's life and 'good enough mothering', and is highly recommended.*

Winnicott DW (1965) *The Family and Individual Development.* London: Tavistock.

Winnicott DW (1971) *Playing and Reality.* Tavistock Publications Ltd.

Winnicott DW (1990) *Deprivation and Delinquency.* Eds: C Winnicott, M Davies and R Shepherd. London: Routledge. *This edited compilation of Winnicott's writing gives more insight into the links between the kind of deprivation experienced and later criminal behaviour.*

# Other titles from Pavilion Publishing

***Mental Health in Intellectual Disabilities: A complete introduction to assessment, intervention, care and support (5th Edition)***
Edited by Colin Hemmings.

Mental Health in Intellectual Disabilities (5th Edition) is a resource for support staff and managers in learning disability services. For more information, visit: www.pavpub.com/learning-disability/ld-mental-health/mental-health-in-intellectual-disabilities-5th-edition

***Guided Self-help for People with Intellectual Disabilities and Anxiety and Depression.*** Edited by Eddie Chaplin.

This booklet is a multi-media training resource that guides facilitators on how to support people with intellectual disabilities. For more information, visit: https://www.pavpub.com/learning-disability/ld-mental-health/guided-self-help

***An Introduction to Supporting the Mental Health of People with Intellectual Disabilities.***
Edited by Eddie Chaplin, Steve Hardy and Karina Marshall-Tate.

A guide for professionals, support staff and families. For more information, visit: https://www.pavpub.com/learning-disability/ld-mental-health/an-introduction-to-supporting-the-mental-health-of-people-with-intellectual-disabilities

***Introduction to Mental Health and Mental Wellbeing for Staff Supporting Adults with Intellectual Disabilities.*** Edited by Eddie Chaplin, Karina Marshall-Tate, Ruwani Trabelsi & Steve Hardy.

This training resource and accompanying reader has been developed for a range of care and support staff who work with adults with intellectual disabilities and provides a full day's training. It aims to provide learners with an understanding of the mental health needs of this population and to promote mental health and wellbeing. For more information, visit: https://www.pavpub.com/mental-health/mental-health-staff-supporting-adults-intellectual-disabilities

***People with Intellectual Disabilities Hear Voices Too.*** By John Cheetham & Nina Melunsky.

A self-study guide for understanding and adapting best practice to support people with intellectual disabilities who hear voices that others cannot hear. For more information, visit: https://www.pavpub.com/learning-disability/people-learning-disabilities-hear-voices

***The CaPDID Training Manual. A Trauma-informed Approach to Caring for People with a Personality Disorder and an Intellectual Disability.***
By Joanna Anderson, Maxwell Pickard & Emma Rye.

This training manual introduces trauma informed approaches to caring for people who have both a personality disorder and an intellectual disability. The CaPDID training is a short course designed for staff without any specific expertise in mental health or psychotherapy, such as care home staff, learning disability nurses, or learning disability care managers.

***Trauma-informed Care in Intellectual Disability. A self-study guide for health and social care support staff.*** By Pat Frankish.

This self-study guide brings together key theories of psychotherapy and disability so that support staff can understand and identify stages of emotional development and plan interventions for the benefit of the person with intellectual disabilities. For more information, visit: https://www.pavpub.com/learning-disability/trauma-informed-care-in-intellectual-disability-a-self-study-guide-for-health-and-social-care-support-staff

***Moss-PAS (ID), Moss-PAS ChA, Moss-PAS Diag(ID), Moss-PAS Check.***
By Dr Steve Moss.

The Moss Psychiatric Assessment Schedules (MPAS) are the successors to the well known PASADD system. The original *Psychiatric Assessment Schedule for Adults with Developmental Disabilities* was developed to provide improved patient interviewing for adults with intellectual disability, and over the years the name became synonymous with mental health assessment in people with intellectual disability. Since those early days, the author has continued to develop new assessments, and to train several thousand people in their use round the world. The insight and feedback from these users has enabled ongoing refinement of the questions, and improvements in the descriptions of symptoms in various levels of severity. The result of this 30 years of development is a set of assessments of unparalleled quality and ease of use.

**The series now includes versions for adults and children, both with intellectual disability, and of normal developmental level.** Coming soon will be an expert interview designed specifically for forensic use. For full information about validity and reliability, together with sample pages to view, visit our PAS-ADD website **www.mosspas.com**